THE
STORY OF
JAMES DOLE

THE STORY OF
JAMES DOLE

By Richard Dole & Elizabeth Dole Porteus

Produced and published by
ISLAND HERITAGE PUBLISHING
A division of the Madden Corporation
99-880 Iwaena Street
Aiea, Hawaii 96701
(808) 487-7299

Designed by Paul Turley

First edition, first printing 1990

CONTENTS

Tending the Wahiawa pineapple fields the old way

PREFACE

by Richard Dole

As I was growing up, every time someone new met me, he or she would immediately ask, "How is business down at the pineapple company?" or something similar. Somehow the name "Dole" was linked with pineapples and with Hawaii.

The story of my grandfather's life and how the DOLE brand name became important was a mystery to me. Family accounts often contradicted and left me confused. The little that was written about him seemed to say the same thing over and over: "He was a young man fresh out of Harvard, who went to Hawaii to seek his fortune." A connection was established between my grandfather and his cousin, Sanford Dole, but it was vague. There was no evidence that Sanford had anything whatsoever to do with my grandfather's business venture. I could never accept the story that Jim Dole raised the money to finance the formation of the Dole Pineapple Company from money raised in the collection plate of his father's church in Boston. Rumors claimed that he lost control of his company during the depression, when he angered the "Big Five" sugar companies by shipping cases of pineapple to the East Coast on Isthmian Lines, at cheaper rates than Matson Navigation Company, a competitor, which was was collectively owned by the "Big Five."

Hawaii is not known as a manufacturing state. Throughout history, only a handful of industries originated nearly from scratch in Hawaii. Pineapple is the largest of these. As a business appraiser and the grandson of the founder of the world pineapple industry, I was curious about just what he did, not only to establish an industry, but to develop a brand name in the process that is one of the major brand names in the food industry, as recognizable as any household food brand in the world today, and one so well associated with quality that food products using it command a price premium over generic ones.

In order to satisfy myself and perhaps learn from his entrepreneurship, I set out to learn just how he put together the pineapple company that bears his name. I needed to trace the history to account for what actually happened.

I was a finance major in college, receiving a B.S. in Finance from the University of Arizona, and continued studying in the area of finance after graduation. I received two professional designations in the area of business analysis - Accredited Senior Appraiser (ASA) and Chartered Financial Analyst (CFA). I've spent my entire career trying to find undervalued publicly- traded stocks, the managing portfolios of securities, the appraisal of a closely-held business enterprise that has no public trading market, or as an agent for a buyer or seller of a business in negotiating a transaction for an entire business.

I've spent over 20 years trying to identify the forces that would influence the value of a business enterprise. I'm associated with Willamette Management Associates, Inc., a pioneer and one of more prestigious business appraisal firms in the country. I'm currently Regional Governor for the Hawaii and Pacific, and Far Eastern Regions of the American Society of Appraisers, and am a Charter Member of the Hawaii Venture Capital Association.

I find that value is qualitative and depends on the eyes of the beholder, on the buyer's and seller's perception of a business enterprise, when trying to decide what the present value of a future stream of benefits might possibly be. Perceptions on outlook change according to economic trends and conditions. I've seen economies and stock markets rise with optimism and fall with fear and I have watched people trying to figure out why it happened.

As a business appraiser, I was particularly impressed with just what my grandfather accomplished in the beginning in forming a highly labor and capital intensive business such as a pineapple company. How did he do it? He had no money. He was trying to promote a product that had been tried before but failed. He was only twenty-four years old and had no business experience. His cousin Sanford Ballard Dole was the Territorial Governor, but my grandfather was new to Hawaii and had no business connections. I tried to identify, not only how he had started the business, but what the "stuff" was that held it all together as the business grew. I looked at the story in relation to Peters and Waterman's book, "In Search of Excellence."

I should have done this book years ago. Unfortunately, my grandfather had a series of strokes before I was twelve years old and I never had a chance to discuss his business with him. I do remember him pointing out oil wells to me when we were driving together somewhere, and he would lecture me about their economic significance. He was always proposing some scheme to me about how to make a dollar on something I had or was doing. At the age of ten, they meant little to me, but I remembered almost everything he told me.

I couldn't find anyone who was around at the time my grandfather started the pineapple company, but he was a prolific writer, and kept a diary and other records through the years. Some of this information is still around. All but one of his children are alive and healthy, and clearly remember growing up with him. Some of his employees and business associates, too, were available for interviews.

I developed the story without any bias or judgments. I only tried to trace his life and highlight his significant achievements. I made no effort to separate his successes and failures.

I wish to offer a special acknowledgement to my wife, Susan, for maintaining patience and encouragement while I conducted my research and documentation on the life of Jim Dole; Elizabeth Dole Porteus (Betty), my aunt and Jim Dole's daughter, who edited and restructured the book in order to make it readable; and Kent Keith, vice president of public relations of Oceanic Properties, who made this book possible.

I would also like to recognize a number of people I interviewed who provided me with valuable information: Terry Sharrer, Ph.D., Smithsonian curator of agriculture; Jack Larsen, pineapple industry consultant; Lex Brodie, former cannery manager and current businessman and small business advocate; Deane Malott, former Hapco vice president and close friend of Jim Dole; Mason Newport, former Dole Foods vice president of operations; Father Robert Mackey, Professor of Business Ethics at Chaminade University; interviews with Charley Dole, Richard A. Dole, Elizabeth Porteus and Barbara Larsen, all children of James D. Dole; David Johnson, a friend of Jim Dole's; Edward Beechert, Ph.D, author of *Working in Hawaii - A Labor History,* published in 1985 by University of Hawaii Press; Paul Brewbaker, associate economist, Bank of Hawaii; Nancy Bush, marketing manager & public affairs assistant, S&W Fine Foods; Karen Johnston, Beatrice/Hunt-Wesson; Thomas Hitch, PH.D; Harry Goff, chairman of the board, Pacific Scientific; James Parker, Dole plantation manager; Chuck Bauman, senior vice president, Dole Foods; Robert Hawthorne, vice president and general manager, Dole Packaged Foods Company; Doug Jocelin, vice president, international, Dole Foods; and Joseph Hartley, president of Maui Pineapple Company.

I was the middle child and first daughter in the James Dole family. When I was growing up, Father was called "The Pineapple King," and I had all the advantages of growing up as a pineapple princess. I lived in a big beautiful house with a cook, a down stairs maid, an upstairs maid, a chauffeur and four yardmen. I had the best of medical and den-

Elizabeth Dole Porteus:

tal care, travelled twice to Europe, and went to private schools (Punahou School and Milton Academy), Vassar College and the Smith College School for Social Work.

Later, when Father was living in San Francisco and I in Honolulu, he would stay with me and my family when he came to town. He had a nice way with the children and we all enjoyed his visits.

Ever since Hebden, my husband, gave me a computer for Christmas some eight years ago, I have been an inveterate word processor user. I wrote up the Dickeys, Mother's side of the family, then the Doles. I rewrote and had published a book I had been working on for years, "My Twentieth Century Philosophy." And I started on a biography of Hebden's father (which is about to be published.)

More than one person suggested that I write about Father, but I never considered doing so. When Richard first thought of writing this book, he asked me if I would do it with him, but I turned him down as I was busy on the biography of Hebden's father. But when he showed me the first part he had finished, I appreciated the tremendous job of research he had done. There were things in it that I didn't know, but since I saw things that seemed to need changing, I told him that I thought I could make it more readable, and he was pleased to have me try.

He sent me the parts as he finished them, I chopped them up, rewrote some, added a little here and there, cut some out, and put the pieces together in new chapters. I would have liked to have more time, but he had a deadline, so I turned over my version to him just before his deadline, and he decided to use it.

A book about Father needed to be written by someone business oriented like Richard. It is his book. I was responsible only for rearranging and polishing it.

FOREWARD

Jim Dole sat in his fourth floor office, his feet on the desk, occasionally scanning a note-pad. Nearby was a box of cigars and to one side an old Panama hat. Next to his desk was a couch specially ordered from the mainland, where he would sometimes take an afternoon nap to break the pace of the day. He paused to look out the window, where over the years he could see steamers come and go with loads of canned pineapples destined for mainland markets.

He had just met with E. I. Bentley, president of California Packing Corporation (C.P.C. or Cal Pac), the predecessor of Del Monte, to talk about a merger between C.P.C. and his company, the Hawaiian Pineapple Co. Ltd. or "Hapco."

Bentley had traveled to Honolulu from San Francisco specifically to scout out the possibilities of an amalgamation. The meeting was only an inquiry, and it was informal but serious. Rumors had already started to buzz around Bishop and Merchant Streets, the financial district of Honolulu. Although no price talks had been released, analysts speculated that in the event the 1928 offer were consummated, the acquisition price would be approximately $75 per share for the 622,716 shares of Hapco outstanding at the end of 1928, or a total of $46.7 million.

This was not the first time a merger or buy-out had been sought. C.P.C. had discussed a merger as early as 1916, and investment bankers and promoters had periodically approached the company about a possible sell-out.

Jim recollected his accomplishments with the pineapple company he had created some 27 years before which had put canned pineapple in every grocery store in the country and had made the name "Hawaiian" almost synonymous with "pineapple." He had written for the 25th reunion class report of his Harvard Class of 1899, "The game has been a very interesting one, taking in practically all the fascinating and troublesome agricultural operations, various transportation questions, and constantly changing manufacturing, marketing and financial problems."

After the company had been incorporated in 1901, the first years had been tough and later years had not been without setbacks, but the company had grown well on its own and current prospects never looked better. It was now the largest producer of pineapple in Hawaii, with 2,750 permanent and 4,250 seasonal employees. It controlled some 33 percent of the market and 60 to 65 percent of all the pineapple land in the islands, over 30,000 to 40,000 acres. 12,000 to 20,000 acres were on Lanai and the remainder in the Wahiawa area of Oahu. The Lanai land was still being developed, and Jim thought that when it was all planted, the company could double its 1928 production.

Earnings per share, adjusted for stock dividends, had increased steadily after 1904 at a compound annual rate of 7.1 percent through 1927, and now in 1928, earnings were up another 78 percent to $3.80 per share. Hapco had paid out regular and sometimes extra cash dividends every year from almost the time it had started showing profits in 1906, the dividend increasing to $2.00 per share in 1928.

Hapco stock traded publicly on the Honolulu Stock Exchange and on the San Francisco Stock Exchange at a high of $57 per share and a low of $42 per share between 1927 and 1928. While it had traded as high as $91 per share in 1920, there had been a number of stock dividends since that date. There had been a 25 percent stock dividend in 1920, a 58 percent one in 1922, a 33-1/3 percent one in 1925, and a 10 percent one in 1927. The result of the stock dividends was to lower the effective price of $90 down to about $39 per share (($90/(1.58 x 1.33 x 1.10) = $38.96). On this basis, the rumored offer price of $75 was more than 30 percent above the adjusted high price of Hapco stock at $57, and Hapco would be selling out or merged at a stock value of nearly 20 times 1928 earnings and 3.5 times sales.

Jim and his board turned down the offer. "The Hawaiian Pineapple Co. is not making and has no intention of making any effort to sell out," Jim said. "It is highly unlikely that the Hawaiian Pineapple Co. would sell out for cash. The company would enter into no merger except upon terms conclusively satisfactory to the stockholders, and which would carry the promise of satisfactory future dealings to distributors, the consuming public and the com-

pany's own employees."

After the C.P.C. offer had been turned down, Hapco was listed for the first time on the New York Stock Exchange on November 30, 1928. The next month, in December, 1928, Charles Head & Company, a stock brokerage firm and a member of both the New York and Boston Stock Exchanges, published a Wall Street investment research report recommending Hawaiian Pineapple Company stock for purchase. It said that the market had room for growth, not only because the 200 million cans per year the pineapple industry was producing only amounted to two cans per person per year in the country, but that foreign market penetration had only just begun.

Jim's was popularly known as the "Pineapple King" and his life was insured by the company for a million dollars. Little did anyone know how soon conditions would change as the Great Depression set in.

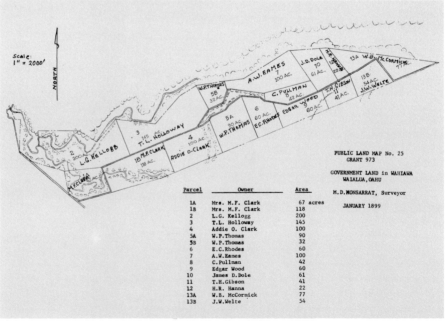

Parcel	Owner	Area
1A	Mrs. M.F. Clark	67 acres
1B	Mrs. M.F. Clark	118
2	L.G. Kellogg	200
3	T.L. Holloway	145
4	Addie O. Clark	100
5A	W.P. Thomas	90
5B	W.P. Thomas	32
6	E.C. Rhodes	60
7	A.W. Eames	100
8	C. Pullman	42
9	Edgar Wood	60
10	James D. Dole	61
11	T.H. Gibson	41
12	H.R. Hanna	22
13A	W.B. McCormick	77
13B	J.W. Welte	54

PUBLIC LAND MAP No. 25
GRANT 973

GOVERNMENT LAND in WAHIAWA
WAIALUA, OAHU

M.D. MONSARRAT, Surveyor

JANUARY 1899

Government land map of Wahiawa-1899

IF

By
RUDYARD KIPLING

If you can keep your head when all about you
Are losing theirs and blaming it on you,
If you can trust yourself when all men doubt you,
But make allowance for their doubting too;
If you can wait and not be tired by waiting,
Or being lied about, don't deal in lies,
Or being hated, don't give way to hating,
And yet don't look too good, nor talk too wise;

If you can dream—and not make dreams your master;
If you can think—and not make thoughts your aim,
If you can meet with Triumph and Disaster
And treat those two imposters just the same;
If you can bear to hear the truth you've spoken
Twisted by knaves to make a trap for fools,
Or watch the things you gave your life to, broken,
And stoop, and build 'em up with worn-out tools;

If you can make one heap of all your winnings
And risk it on one turn of pitch-and-toss,
And lose, and start again at your beginnings
And never breathe a word about your loss;
If you can force your heart and nerve and sinew
To serve your turn long after they are gone,
And so hold on when there is nothing in you
Except the Will which says to them: "Hold on."

If you can talk with crowds and keep your virtue,
Or walk with Kings—nor lose the common touch,
If neither foes nor loving friends can hurt you,
If all men count with you, but none too much;
If you can fill the unforgiving minute
With sixty seconds' worth of distance run,
Yours is the Earth and everything that's in it,
And—which is more—you'll be a Man, my son!

(A favorite poem of James Dole)

Family Background

Charley, Jim, Betty, Dick, Barbara, Belle and Jimmy about 1918

The Dole name is supposed to have come from a little town in northwestern France named Dol, and a Hugues de Dol, who left France with William the Conqueror to invade England, is supposed to be the ancestor of the Doles in England.

The first Dole to arrive in America was Richard Dole, who was born in the early sixteen hundreds in a village near Bristol, England, named Ringwothy (or Rangeworthy). In 1637, his father apprenticed him for seven years as a merchant clerk to John Lowle, a Glover and probably a cousin. When John Lowle sailed with other Puritans to America in 1639, Richard went with him, and they settled in Newbury, Massachusetts, about forty miles north of Boston.

After his seven years apprenticeship

was up, Richard went into business for himself as a merchant.

His shop was on a bay near the mouth of a river, where he did business with clipper ships sailing into the harbor and with the boats that brought produce down from the country up-river. His business flourished and in time he owned a tannery, a still, and considerable real estate. Included in his estate when he died were slaves whom, under the terms of his will, he released after his death. Richard and his wife Hanna, whom he married in 1647, are supposed to be the ancestors of all the Doles in America. They had ten children, and Jim was descended from the tenth, Abner.

One of Abner's great-great-grandsons, Wigglesworth Dole, a farmer like so many Americans at the time, was

Jim's great-grandfather. Wigglesworth had a daughter, Elizabeth, and three sons, Daniel, Nathan (Jim's grandfather), and Isaiah. Isaiah was a teacher and librarian. Elizabeth did not marry, but moved in with Isaiah after his wife died and brought up his children. Both Daniel and Nathan were Congregational ministers.

The Reverend Daniel Dole, born Sept. 9, 1808, graduated from Bowdoin College in 1836 and Bangor Theological Seminary in 1839 and was ordained into the Congregationalist ministry the next year. After his marriage to Emily H. Ballard, a school principal, the couple sailed out of Boston around Cape Horn for Hawaii (then known as the Sandwich Islands) to be missionaries. The following year, Daniel became the first principal of Punahou School, created to educate the missionary children. Dole Street in Honolulu was named after him. Daniel and Emily had two children, George Hathaway and Sanford Ballard. George, who left the islands to live in Riverside, California, had thirteen children. Sanford, about whom we will hear more later, had none, but became a historic figure in Hawaii.

The Rev. Nathan Dole, Jim's grandfather, was born May 8, 1811 in Bloomfield, now Skowhegan, Maine. He graduated from Bowdoin College in 1836 and from Bangor Theologial Seminary in 1841, and was ordained as pastor of the first Congregational Church in Brewer, Maine, in 1842. Unfortunately, he died of consumption when he was only forty-four. After his death, his wife, Caroline Fletcher Dole, took Charles, ten, and his younger brother, Nat, barely three, back to Norridgewock, Maine, to live with her mother, Mrs. Amos Fletcher in the big Fletcher home.

Caroline was very religious and maintained a strict no-frills Calvinist home. She was a scholar and poet and took charge of the education of her sons. Her greatest desire was for her boys to be Christians and to devote themselves to the service of God, and she expected Charles to be either a minister or a missionary.

Nathan and Caroline's son, Charles, Jim's father, was born on May 17, 1845 in Brewer, Maine. He attended a one-room school in Norridgewock but was educated mostly by his mother. On Sundays he attended two sermons at church, a Sunday School session in between, and a prayer meeting in the evening. From Saturday night to Monday morning he was allowed no amusements whatsoever and only religious reading.

Charles was born just a year after his cousin Sanford was born in Hawaii. While he was growing up, he often wrote to his Hawaiian cousins, and exchanged cracked butternuts and maple sugar for sea shells, coral, and lava. When Sanford came to Massachusetts to finish his education at Williams College, they became friends. Once the cousins went for a camping trip in Maine. Sanford became sick and when Charles tried to find a shortcut back, they became lost. They ended up lifelong friends.

During the Civil war, when Charles was sixteen, he served in the militia, and one of his assignments was to guard a fort in Maine from an attack from the Confederacy. He went on to Harvard, where he graduated Summa Cum Laude in 1868 and earned a Master's degree in 1871. He taught school for a year in Boston, but his mother's religious influence was so ingrained in him, that he decided to be a minister, and he entered the Andover Theological Seminary, from which he graduated the following year.

From the beginning, Charles was an independent thinker. As a boy going to Church he wondered why Jesus was better than any other man who had died for his country or for his beliefs. He continued to think for himself throughout his schooling. After he had graduated from the Seminary, his independent thinking stood in the way when he tried to find a church. Most of the Congregational churches had creeds and insisted that their ministers subscribe to them. Now not only did Charles find that they were creeds which he could not accept, but he had too much integrity to subscribe to what he did not believe. Unable at first to find a church, he took a position as professor of Greek at the University of Vermont.

While a junior at Harvard, Charles had met and fallen in love with Frances Drummond, the daughter of his father's Bowdoin roommate. They were married while he was with the University of Vermont.

The following year, some church elders who had known Charles' father, decided to overlook his refusal to agree completely with the creed of their church and invited him to be their minister. He was thereupon ordained as a Congregational minister at the Plymouth Church in Portland, Maine, in 1874.

Two years later, in 1876, he left the Plymouth Church to be the pastor of the First Congregational Church of Jamaica Plain, a suburb of Boston. Though Congregational in name, this was actually a Unitarian Church and well suited to Charles' way of thinking.

Unitarianism, which evolved in America from a liberal branch of the New England Congregational Church, began in New England in the 1740's, took hold in Harvard in 1805, and was associated with many humanitarian efforts. It was not "Christian," by definition, because, although it maintained the ethics of Christianity, it did not believe in the divinity of Christ. An early leader was William Ellery Channing, minister of Boston's Federal Street Church, who had considerable influence on Ralph Waldo Emerson, Henry Wadsworth Longfellow and others.

Although her father had been a Unitarian, Caroline, Charles' mother, had all her life considered Unitarians infidels, so for Charles to become the minister of a Unitarian Church was a shock to her. Years later, as Charles wrote, he "turned to his mother and said, 'Mother, if Nathan (his brother) and I had gone as missionaries to Africa and been eaten by crocodiles, you would feel happier about us, wouldn't you?' A sad little smile played about her mouth, while by her silence she gave her plain answer 'Yes' to my proposition."

Charles continued to be an independent thinker and never hesitated to say what he thought. He is considered by the Unitarians as one of their outstanding thinkers of the time. He was a proponent of civil rights and women's suffrage, and was a critic of immorality in the government. Although his family had been Whigs, and he became a Republican, he thought party affiliations were shallow, and he thought of himself as an Independent. While a non-drinker, he was against prohibition, and he favored divorce to irreconcilable marital differences.

Charles was a pacifist during World War I and was outraged that other churches, especially Unitarian ones, did not speak out against war. He said the churches "were accepting the ancient piece of easy heathenism, that you may do evil that good may come, that you can stop fighting by fighting and stop killing by more killing; in short, you can use Satan to cast out Satan. As for their Golden Rule, they did not believe it would work!"

He joined organizations in which he believed, such as the World Peace Foundation. He served as president of the Association to Abolish War, as vice-president of the Anti-Imperialistic League and as a director of the American Peace Society.

Charles' religion was based on a philosophy of "Good Will," as he writes in

Belle Dickey Dole's wedding day, Nov. 26, 1906

his autobiography, "My Eighty Years," the last of his twenty-five publications: "Through the strife of fighting wills and in all human history runs like a cable the line of one grand stable will. It is the will of the Master of Life. It always moves toward the truth, and toward justice, constituting the welfare of all men. It is dynamic and always new. This is God's will, the Good Will working in all to make the individual link the power of his little will to the great Good Will, and the infinite resources of the universe will flow through his life...Let anyone try it, and see for himself. We never know satisfaction, restfulness, freedom, except when we trust ourselves and all that we have in going the way of the Good Will."

Charles was a loving father to Jim and continued through his life to advise him and help him whenever he could. Many of his letters may be found in Jim's files, counseling and guiding him when he was struggling with both money and supply problems in his efforts to start his pineapple company. When Jim was trying to pack his first crop of pineapple in 1903, Charles wrote: "..don't take the business too seriously, laugh every day, use your philosophy and see that it

becomes a religion for your comfort and uplift. A man needs a bit of quieting thought every day, that he may do his work more effectively. It is quite as necessary as food in order to keep his nerves from jarring."

Charles continued at the Jamaica Plain church, much beloved by his rather well-to-do congregation until he retired as Emeritus in 1916, after which he continued to preach until he was over eighty. One of those who attended his church was Ulysses S. Grant. In 1906 he was granted a doctorate (S.D.T.) by Bowdoin College. He died in November, 1927.

Jim's mother, Frances Drummond Dole, or "Fannie," as Charles called her, was born on February 4, 1846 in Auburn, Maine. She was the daughter of the Rev. James Drummond and Esther Anne Swett Drummond. Her father the Rev. James Drummond had been a roommate of Nathan, Charles' father, when they were both attending Bowdoin College. Both contracted tuberculosis at college and died young. Charles and Fannie first met as children. They met again when he was a junior at Harvard, and she was staying in Sommerville, Mass., taking singing lessons from a noted orchestra leader. This time he fell in love with her and after a long courtship and a four year engagement, they were married on March 4, 1873, while Charles was teaching at the University of Vermont.

Fannie and Charles both loved Maine and they built a summer home in Southwest Harbor. The house was on a hillside, with a trail to the sound below, where there was a pier to moor their boats. Jim and his brother and sister spent their summers sailing, while Fannie tended her flower garden and painted scenes of Maine.

Jim wrote about the place later when he was 79: "A few words about this 100 miles of Maine, separated from the con-

Jim Dole's family, photo taken in 1911, includes Richard, James, Elizabeth and his wife Belle

tinent by a narrows and pretty well covered with little granite mountains running up to 1530 feet; a lake between nearly every pair of mountains and a trout brook running into nearly every lake, the island (Mt. Desert Island) cut nearly in two by the fiord-like Somes Sound; the island surrounded with granite ledges and sea walls and penetrated by numerous coves and harbors. A lovely play ground." Some of the men he later took to Hawaii to work with him were friends he had known in Southwest Harbor, such as Fred Tracy and John Whitmore.

There were no laws at the time restricting loggers from cutting down the fir trees on the island. Concerned about this, Fannie lobbied with the Maine legislature for laws to make the Mt. Desert forests into a state park.

Fannie inherited sizable portions of the estates of three of her uncles, and was well off. She bought heirloom furniture, jewelry, always had a maid, and was generous in her donations to charitable institutions, but she had a thrifty streak that led her to buy the cheapest types of meat, such as sweetbreads and brains, which the butcher saved for her, and to instill thriftiness in her children. Frances' grandaughter, Betty, remembers the shapeless sweaters which she sent as gifts, which she had knit with big needles and never fit.

After Jim was established in Hawaii, his parents visited frequently. Her grandchildren in Hawaii remembered "Grandma Dole" as frank, critical and rather cold. On one of her first trips, she was horrified at the way Belle was bringing up the children, and persuaded Jim to hire a strict German nanny, which turned out to be a mistake as the boys rebelled at her discipline.

Frances died three years after the death of her husband, in 1930, at the age of 84.

This combination of strict and critical mother and doting father seems to be a good one sometimes for producing children who are full of self-confidence and drive to succeed

Charles and Frances had four children. Jim was the oldest, Katherine was next but died a year after she was born. Following Katherine was Winifred and then Richard.

Winifred (Win) was born on March 5, 1882. She, too, spent her summers sailing at Southwest Harbor and, like her mother, painting. She was a sociable person with many friends. After she visited her cousins, the George Doles, in Riverside, California, George wrote that she was "a very jolly girl, and is always boiling over with her exuberant spirits...She seems to me like a genuine child of nature, so utterly unaffected, so spontaneous, so unspoiled by fashion." Her niece, Barbara Larsen, Jim's youngest daughter, enjoyed Win particularly because she was "fun loving." She was outgoing, warm and athletic, and even liked to swim without anything on. "She had a marvelous sense of humor," Barbara's sister, Betty, said, "and always enjoyed everyone's attempts to be funny, even if they didn't seem funny to others." She and Jim were very fond of each other throughout their lives.

Perhaps Win's appreciation of Jim's early attempts to be funny stimulated him to develop the ability to tell jokes and make people laugh, which was so much a part of his personality all his life.

When Jim was starting his pineapple business, Win came to visit. While in Honolulu, she stayed mostly with Sanford and Anna, but of course saw a lot of Jim. After her return to New England, she married Horace Mann, a grandson of Horace Mann, the famous educator. Horace was a teacher at Mil-

Frances Drummond, Jim's mother

ton Academy until he lost his hearing in an automobile accident.

Winifred and Horace had two daughters, Katherine and Barbara. The family lived in Richmond in the Massachusetts Berkshires, but continued to spend their summers at the Dole home in Southwest Harbor in Maine.

When Charles and Fannie died, they left the Maine house to Win, and she enjoyed it for many years, and often hosted Jim and other members of his family there. After she decided to live in Southwest Harbor through the winters as well as the summers, she sold it, and bought another house closer to town. She died there in 1978, at the age of 96.

Richard D. Dole, (Dick) the youngest of Charles and Frances' children, was born on July 9, 1884. He loved Southwest Harbor and sailing, and had his own boat when he was sixteen. Since he was so interested in the sea and little interested in school work, his father decided that he might be happiest with a career at sea, so he signed him up in 1900 to work as a merchant marine apprentice on one of the Standard Oil sailing vessels shipping oil to the Orient. Unfortunately, on his first trip, Dick came down with dysentery after leaving Shanghai and died on August 12, 1901, at the age of 17, and was buried at sea.

Edgar J. Walker, manager of The Hawaiian Feed and Coffee Co., an importer and exporter of coffee in Hilo, wrote Jim about meeting one of the sailors on the "Astrol," Dick's ship, when it docked in Honolulu. The sailor said that everyone on the ship had had dysentery, but Dick was the only one who failed to recover. He said that Dick was well liked by captain and crew, and all grieved his death.

JIM'S BOYHOOD

Charles F. Dole and James, about 1882

James Drummond Dole (Jim) was born in Jamaica Plain, Mass., a suburb of Boston, on September 27, 1877. A few days after he was born, an old man who had lost a son, brought a gift of $50 for him. This was the beginning of the savings account which Jim used when he first set out for Hawaii in 1899 to seek his fortune.

While growing up, Jim was athletic. When he was in college, he was tall and lanky, just under 6 feet tall and weighed a little over 120 pounds. His sport, besides sailing, was the high jump. In 1895, he jumped 5'7" and placed second in a track meet. He was also an avid ice skater, sometimes spending three or four hours at a time on the ice.

Music was not his gift. A story he liked to tell later was of how, when more singers were needed for a chorus of 500 to sing at the Boston Conservatory of Music, he thought it was his duty to volunteer, but after an interview in which he demonstrated how little he knew about music, instead of being put in the chorus, he was offered a position as usher. He loved to sing, but often his singing was a bit off key.

Jim's father, Charles, nevertheless, had a high opinion of him. In his autobiography, "My Eighty Years," Charles wrote that Jim "had plenty of nerve-force, which, most likely, makes a strong will." He also wrote, "Jim did not specially shine as a scholar, but we were never worried over this. The processes of his mind were straightforward and he possessed good common sense." And again, "Jim developed admirable qualities of courage and resourcefulness...He learned readily to adjust himself, with kindly respect, to the intercourse with various human characters. No school could do better as regards these fundamental points of education. He was not precocious enough to reveal for what kind of work in the world he was likely to be useful. Morally, he never gave us the slightest anxiety."

Jim attended Roxbury Latin School in Boston and then went on to Harvard in 1895, from which he graduated in 1899 with an A.B. degree. During his four years at Harvard, he received four B's, and eight C's for his courses, and one A, two B's, eight C's, and two D's in his half-courses. The only A he received was for a half-course in botany during his freshmen year.

With his friendliness and sense of fun, Jim was popular and made many friends. He and a number of his classmates lived together in the same house at Harvard, near where the "Broadway Electric" train "rushed by" at night. Jim continued to correspond with his Harvard friends after he went to Hawaii, and many of them helped him finance his pineapple company.

During his summers at Southwest Harbor, Jim developed an interest in horticulture, growing corn, beans and other vegetables in his mother's garden. When he had taken enough courses at Harvard to graduate and was free to take elective non-credit courses, he enrolled in the Bussey Institution, Harvard's School of Agriculture and Horticulture, one of Harvard's research institutes, and the only curriculum Harvard had to offer in agricultural science. During this last year at Harvard, he spent the bulk of his time at Bussey.

The Bussey Institution was not far from where Jim lived, as it was on the border of Jamaica Plain, near the Providence Railroad station. It was funded by a foundation set up under the Will of Benjamin Bussey. The purpose of the school was to give "systematic instruction in Agriculture, and in Useful and Ornamental Gardening." It was basically separate from Harvard College, as it had its own admission and graduation

requirements. Not all of the students were from Harvard, although students at Harvard interested in agricultural science were encouraged to attend. Graduation requirements from the Bussey, if not otherwise enrolled at

Winifred and Richard

Harvard, required courses in chemistry, botany, physics, mathematics, biology, geography, geology, meteorology, drawing, French, and German. Since Jim was already enrolled and near graduation at Harvard and had taken classes in botany, mathematics, geology, and French at Harvard and German at Roxbury Latin School, he did not have to take the general courses.

Bussey had courses in irrigation, crop rotation, special crops and farms. There were also courses in the theory and practice of farming and horticulture. The Dean, Professor Francis H. Storer, taught agricultural chemistry. Instruction emphasized practical applications. Included in the program were lectures and lab work in greenhouses and fields, where experiments were conducted. Jim learned how to prepare land for farming, harvest crops, and how to select the proper agricultural and food processing equip-

Jim's children, Barbara, Charley, Betty, Jimmy and Dick, about 1919

ment, and how to apply "scientific literature."

One of the most useful things Jim learned at the Bussey was the study of the technology used in the "preservation of meat, apples, pears, cranberries, and other fruits." He also learned how to construct and implement the appropriate buildings housing these facilities. When he started on his pineapple processing venture, he was already aware of all the scientific achievement in the field, and was probably better prepared for it than anyone else in the Islands.

After Jim had graduated from Harvard and Bussey, a decision had to be made as to what he would do next.

Hawaii had been much in the news while Jim was growing up, and all the more interesting to him and his family because their cousin, Sanford Ballard Dole, was so much involved. Cousin Sanford was part of the group which overthrew the Queen in 1893. When the new leaders set up a Provisional Government, they chose Sanford to be the President. They asked the United States to annex Hawaii, but President Cleveland thought Hawaii should be re-

turned to the Queen. When the United States turned down their bid for annexation, they established the Republic of Hawaii in 1894, and Sanford was again the President. In 1898 there was a new movement for annexation, and now, not only was the new United States president, President McKinley, favorable toward annexation, but the United States had discovered the military importance of Hawaii during the Spanish-American war.

It was during Jim's 1898 summer vacation that Hawaii became a Territory of the United States. The House of Representatives passed the resolution for annexation on June 15th, the Senate on July 6th and the President signed it on July 7th, and on August 12th the ceremony was held in Hawaii for the transfer of sovereignty, with the formal annexation of Hawaii to the United States to take place later.

Charles did not approve of Sanford and his group taking the government of Hawaii away from the Hawaiian Queen, and he wrote Sanford of his opposition, but their friendship and correspondence continued.

Once, when Sanford was visiting Jim's family in New England, Jim overheard him and his father discussing a pamphlet published in 1893, the year the Hawaiian monarchy fell, written by Joseph Marsden, then the agricultural commissioner of Hawaii, who had been hired as a public relations man to promote small coffee farms in Hawaii. The economy of Hawaii was based solely on sugar, and Marsden hoped that other crops could be developed so that Hawaii would not be dependent on a single agricultural commodity. Trying to attract "white farmers," the pamphlet told about Hawaii for Jim. Sanford's answer was that he might seek employment on one of the sugar plantations.

Jim spent the summer after college at Southwest Harbor, sailing and racing his boat "Curlen" with his brother, Dick, and his childhood friend, Fred Tracy, and sometimes Jim's sister, Win, joined them as crew. At the end of the summer, he made up his mind to go to Hawaii. He sold his sailboat for $94, and for extra cash, he sold some shares of stock he owned to his father, who then gave them to his brother and sister. These sales supplemented his $1,200 savings

Rev. Charles Fletcher Dole, Jim's father

Frances Drummond Dole, Jim's mother

waii's abundant resources and low cost homestead land. Other possible crops were rubber, coffee, sisal, and fruits, including pineapple.

This discussion set Jim to thinking. Since New England was becoming more industrial than agricultural, he began to wonder if Hawaii would be a better place to pursue his agricultural career. Some of his friends at college thought so and other Boston friends, when consulted, thought it a good idea for him to work for a year in Hawaii as an apprentice to gain practical agricultural experience. Charles wrote Sanford to find out what opportunities there would be in

account at Providential National Savings, which had been started when he was a boy. His father agreed to manage the account and to forward money to him as needed. Jim next met with the editor of the "Transcript," a New England newspaper, about the possibility of publishing some articles about Hawaii. He also bought a pair of pruning shears and a book on bookkeeping.

While in Boston, Jim met two men who were living in Hawaii who happened to be visiting. One was Walter Dillingham, two years his senior and another Harvard alumnus, who later was to be important in relation to Jim's

CHAPTER TWO

pineapple business. The other was Joseph (Joe) Brewer, a relative of Edward M. and Helen S. Brewer, who were friends of Jim's family, and possibly members of his father's church. Brewer said he would introduce Jim to the Castles of Castle & Cooke, Inc., an agent to the sugar plantations, which might offer him a job as a bookkeeper. He recommended bookkeeping as a way to gain knowledge of the costs associated with producing sugar. He also suggested that Jim look up Albert Judd Jr. He gave Jim five letters of introduction to men in Hawaii who might help him get a job when he arrived.

Jim had at least $1,500 in ready cash, which doesn't seem like much today, but based on a complex formula developed on January 17, 1989 by Paul Brewbaker, an associate economist of the Bank of Hawaii, who, using data from the Bureau of Labor Statistics and the Consumer Price Index, estimated that, since the Consumer Price Index was 8.4 from 1900 to 1901 as compared to 120.3 in Nov. 1988, one of Jim's dollars would buy approximately $14.33 today. His $1,500 would therefore be worth $21,495 in 1988 dollars. That was quite enough for a thrifty young Yankee to get started, and it put him in a position to scout out all sorts of possibilities without being forced to take the first job that came along.

Jim's friends in Boston were full of ideas as to what he might grow in Hawaii. One thought he should grow lilies, another, coffee. Jim became interested in coffee when he heard that, while Hawaiian coffee was retailing for $.35 per lb. in New England, one could grow it for $.08 a pound and sell it for $.18 a pound. (Later he found that the high price was due to a 35% tariff on the importation of coffee from the Islands into the U.S.)

Commenting on his early plans some years later, Jim said, "I got the notion that life in Hawaii was just one long, sweet song. I had the idea that after two or three years of reasonable effort expended on cheap government land, I would be able to spend the rest of my life in a hammock, smoking cigars rolled from tobacco grown on my own place, and generally enjoying a languorous life of ease and plenty."

Roxbury Latin School, class of 1895. Jim standing, fourth from right

Off To Hawaii

An effort to control bubonic plague in Chinatown by fire, resulted in its destruction

Jim's liberal arts education at Harvard, horticulture training at the Bussey, a background in New England thrift and his Unitarian upbringing all helped prepare him for the enterprise he was about to develop. It also helped prepare him to avoid the traps that snare young men who venture out from home for the first time.

Jim's first major challenge was in San Francisco, where, after a long train trip across the country, he was waiting for his ship to depart and an old street-wise man, thinking that he had a sucker, lured him into a poker game. Jim planned to include this event in an autobiography he started in his later years, but never got past his notes. Justice couldn't be given to the story without quoting much of it directly:

"By this time I wished myself safely out on the street but didn't know how best to bring this to pass. It was no surprise when one of the four strangers replaced the gambling gear and suggested a friendly game of poker. I explained that I couldn't afford to risk money at cards and had no job and no income. An argument followed, and one of the men, saying "Let's try one," dealt a hand around the table, taking pains to give me an unbeatable hand, evidently with the aim of leading me to taste success and acquiesce in a game. How I should best have extricated myself from the situation I have never decided, but this is what happened: I covered the bet, won, picked up my own original money (the money on the table was all in gold pieces, as was most of the money in San Francisco banks and pockets in those days, with the exception of the tons of silver cartwheels), pushed the rest of the money back to the middle of the table and said, 'I told you I didn't want to play. I don't want to lose my money or win yours.' I put on my hat, rose, walked to the door, downstairs and out into the

23

welcome sunlight of the street, unslugged, unshot, with no further word from anyone, but such a disagreeable taste in my mouth as I have never experienced before or since.

Something said in the conversation before the game started led me to suspect that one of the four strangers was from Honolulu and this, together with my having not unwillingly admitted that my father was a cousin of Sanford B. Dole, head of the Hawaiian Provisional Government which overthrew Queen Liliokulani in 1893, President of the Republic of Hawaii not only until Hawaii was annexed to the United States by joint resolution of Congress in 1898, but until Hawaii's Territorial Government took effect by the Organic Act of July 1, 1900, led me to guess that perhaps my escape, unscathed, may have been due to this circumstance. This guess was slightly strengthened by my seeing in Honolulu, repeatedly, a man who, I think, was one of the four. Never, however, was I sure enough to whisper the possibility of the identity I suspected."

Jim first arrived in Hawaii on November 16, 1899, a slim young man about 5'11-1/2" tall and weighing 130 lbs. He moved in with his Cousin Sanford and his wife Anna. One of the first things he did was to buy a Panama hat.

The second week Jim was in Hawaii, there was an outbreak of bubonic plague and a six month quarantine. He watched the fire department attempt to disinfect an area of one or two blocks of Chinatown on a windy day by starting a fire, which got out of hand and burned Chinatown to the ground. There was almost a riot in Chinatown because the quarantined residents thought that they were intentionally placed in a detention area to be burned up.

During the quarantine, Jim spent much of his time loafing on the beach near Sanford's Honolulu home, and reading. He read Hamlet, King Lear, Henry VIII and other books, often reading them aloud to his Cousin Anna.

Jim's friends in New England were jealous of his life in the tropics while they were fighting the snow in Boston. Page Wheelright, a Jamaica Plain friend wrote: "I imagine this will sound strange to you as you sit fanning yourself in the shade of a palm tree..." There was no problem reaching him. One simply addressed the letter to "Mr. James D. Dole, Honolulu, Hawaiian Islands, c/o President Dole."

It was while Jim was staying with Sanford and Anna that Hawaii was formally annexed as a Territory to the U.S., on "Inauguration Day, Territory of Hawaii," June 14, 1900, and Sanford was elected Governor. Jim wrote about some of the events in his diary: "June 14 was a gala day in the Islands...In the morning the Inauguration exercises took place on the Makai steps of the capital. Cousin Sanford in a Prince Albert and stovepipe looked finely and read his address well...In the evening, I stayed out and appeared at the Inauguration Ball, which was quite a swell affair." Jim claimed that Sanford didn't really want to be governor, but ran for the position to make sure at least one of his opponents didn't get in.

Jim earned some money after he arrived in Hawaii writing articles about Hawaii. One, the "Hawaiian Political Broil," published in the Boston Transcript was about Sanford's role in the Annexation. Jim felt that Sanford was given a lot of bad press during this period, and it is assumed that his own article was more favorable to Sanford. He sent a copy to Anna, Sanford's wife, for her approval.

After Jim had been in Hawaii for over a month without a job, Sanford offered him $1.00 a day to trim his algaroba trees. This Jim was well equipped to do with his new pruning shears.

Sanford also encouraged Jim to check out the Waialua sugar plantation for employment, which he did. From the visit he learned the costs for labor and for clearing land in Hawaii, knowledge that was later helpful to him. He then met with Charles M. Cooke, president of the Ewa Plantation Company, an affiliated sugar plantation in Ewa. Some time later, he met William R. Castle and Edward D. Tenney, both on the board of directors of Castle & Cooke, who suggested that he visit the Ewa Plantation. None of these visits, however, led to a job.

Sanford B. Dole

Instead of becoming an employee of a sugar company, Jim bought stock first in Ewa Plantation and then Waialua Agricultural Co. After four-and-a-half months, he sold his 50 shares of Ewa Plantation at a gain of 21%, which brought in nearly $1,500 cash, which he invested in Waialua Agriculture Co.

The idea of farming for himself appealed more to Jim anyway than working for others, and he still was interested in farming, so he was on the lookout for land to farm. This might seem a rather foolish choice to us today but the period after the Spanish American War to after World War I was the best time in history for farmers. It has been called the "Golden Age of American Agriculture." It was a time when agricultural prices were rising faster than production costs.

Jim soon found that there was little land available for sale anywhere on Oahu. The last sale was one of 65 acres for $125,000, on a site which was soon expected to advance to $5,000 per acre.

Then, on April 30, 1900, Sanford told him about a 61 acre tract of land in Wahiawa, 23 miles from Honolulu, which the current owner had relinquished to the government and which was to be put up for sale at a public auction.

Sanford had heard about it from Byron O. Clark, who owned about 200 acres in Wahiawa. Clark was primarily responsible for the early pineapple plantations in Wahiawa. He had been a fruit farmer in California, and upon arriving in Hawaii in 1897, had become the Commissioner of Agriculture for the Republic of Hawaii. While holding that position, he found that most of the land in Hawaii was held by private individuals, and was expensive to buy or lease. Land in Wahiawa was an exception, for it had been designated as homestead land by the Land Act of 1895, which provided that certain government land would become available for sale once its leases expired. President Dole, himself, had shown him the Wahiawa land.

The Land Act stipulated that an association of settlers could purchase the land, provided that they were willing to live on the land and farm it for a minimum of three years. The tract included a total of 1,300 acres. With annexation pending, Clark realized that he must act quickly, because a change in the law might follow annexation. He was able to obtain a one year option from the Land Commission to form an association and to purchase the Wahiawa tract. He and a number of California friends and acquaintances then formed the "Wahiawa Colony Tract" and an agricultural coop-

25   CHAPTER THREE

Honolulu Harbor-1900

erative called the "Hawaiian Fruit and Plant Company" to grow fresh food products for the Hawaiian and West Coast markets.

Clark thereupon packed up his family in Southern California and moved out to Wahiawa to be a farmer. The land was divided into plots of 20 acres for each family member. Included originally were thirteen families totalling eighty people. They cleared the land in late 1898 and planted oranges, limes, grapes, grapefruit, melons, bananas, sugar cane, peaches, figs, pears, avocados, pineapples, wheat, and barley.

Clark invited Jim to see the land. He told him that several people had already expressed an interest in it and he suggested that Jim quickly file an application. The land was one of the higher elevation sites, which Clark felt would be suitable for growing pineapples or bananas.

The next day Jim met Clark and his brother-in-law Leonard G. Kellogg, the manager of the Hawaiian Fruit & Plant Co., in Honolulu, who told him that water would be available if needed. Kellogg showed him a map of the property and explained how he planned to dam up the creek below, and to supply water to both the Waialua Agricultural Co. and the Wahiawa settlement, and sell the balance.

Jim considered his alternatives: "(1) It will enable me to go to work much sooner than anything else, (2) The place is near Honolulu and therefore within reach of people and within fair distances of a large and increasing market for produce of various kinds, especially poultry and pineapples, peas and other vegetables which the Chinamen do not raise successfully. The drawbacks are that it is not the sort of pioneer life that I had rather in my mind. It is apt to be a rather narrow life." He was not clear how red dirt farming fit in with his training in horticulture at the Bussey. Nor did he think that the opportunity for income in Wahiawa would be as great as they might be some other place, as perhaps on the Big Island of Hawaii growing lilies. Still, here he could use

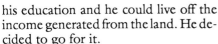

(Above) Byron O. Clark and Capt. John Kidwell

his education and he could live off the income generated from the land. He decided to go for it.

Now Jim began to wonder if he had sufficient funds to buy the property if others bid aggressively when it came up for auction. He recalled that James Green, a friend of his father in Boston and possibly a member of his father's church, had offered to lend him money if he needed it while in Hawaii. Now that the opportunity to buy the sixty-one acre Wahiawa tract came up, Jim immediately wrote his father about taking up Green's offer or anyone else's for $2,000. His father was able to get the $2,000, not from James Green, but from Charles Bowditch, probably another member of his church. With this extra money, Jim felt prepared to enter the forthcoming auction.

In spite of his need for cash at the time, Jim loaned his Chinese friend and houseboy at Sanford's home, Ah Lim, $300 for seven months to open up a store and coffee shop. This act of generosity proved helpful later when Ah Lim helped supply Jim's Wahiawa plantation with labor.

The government homestead auction for the Wahiawa tract was held on July 28, 1900. The price quickly moved up to $3,000, with Jim and another man named Hendrick bidding. Jim finally got it at $4,000, which was much more than he had expected. Nevertheless, he was pleased and so was Sanford. But now he was short of cash and wrote his father to see if he could borrow some more money from Bowditch, Green or anyone else.

In less than two months from the end of the bubonic plague quarantine, Jim Dole now had three lots totalling 61 acres. He moved from Sanford's Honolulu home to Wahiawa, where he stayed with the Clarks until he could build a shack. As he wrote later, "I took up my residence thereon as a farmer, unquestionably of the 'dirt' variety."

Farming At Wahiawa

Jim and Fred Tracy on the original homestead at Wahiawa in 1901

Jim's Wahiawa land, when he bought it, was covered with wild grass and guava bushes with no improvements whatsoever on it. There were not the trees that are there now, so he could see the ocean on both the Honolulu and Waialua sides of the island. He started by building a barn, and after leaving the Clarks' home, he slept in the barn until he could build a one-room shack. He often told later about how a hen would come in to lay eggs on a shelf.

One of the first things Jim did was to go to the Honolulu stockyards and purchase a horse, which he named "Withers," after the seller. Withers had been a runaway, had a cracked hoof, but was a good horse, according to Jim. The problem was that he scarcely knew anything about riding a horse. He used to joke later that as a sailor, he thought Withers had to be tied both fore and aft.

Withers moved into the barn with him. Jim's first equipment consisted of "Withers," his horse, a wagon, a plow, a harrow, a name, and a New England accent.

It wasn't long before Jim faced his first Kona storm. As the wind blew, the new home shook back and forth. Abandoning the shack, he ran out into the night to the security of the barn. When he heard sheets of iron blowing off the house roof of his neighbor, Alfred W. Eames, he realized that his other neighbor, Thomas H. Gibson and his wife, who had babies, might need help. As he sloshed through the mud to their house, he noticed that every time the wind blew, the roof was lifted up a foot at a time. When he got to the house, he helped Gibson lash down the roof with a rope. He later learned that another Wahiawa pioneer, Dr. Emmit Rhodes and his wife, held their home together by tying a rope to the roof, taking the rope to bed with them and hanging on all night.

Jim's friends and family were intrigued by his decision to move to a sixty acre plantation in Wahiawa, twenty-five miles from town. When a Harvard classmate, George Damon Dutton, heard about it, he wrote, "I have a picture of you wearing a great straw hat with a flopping brim and straddling your little native horse, as you ride to town to get this letter." He wrote again: "It seems an ideal life going about in a shirt and an old hat, I suppose." Jim's sister, Winifred, named her row-boat "Wahiawa." Most of her friends called it "Wah! Wah!" and the boat became known by that name up and down the New England coast.

About a year after Jim arrived in Hawaii, Fred Tracy, the friend with whom Jim had so often sailed at Southwest Harbor, moved to the Islands to join him. Fred had written Jim before he had bought the Wahiawa property, asking if he could join him, and Jim had answered that Hawaii was not a resort, but it would be O.K. as long as he didn't bring his cousin Merle along. Before moving to Hawaii, Tracy had worked at his father's dairy in Southwest Harbor running a "mowing machine." Another New England friend, Fred Mayo, wasn't so sure that Tracy would be an asset.

At the beginning, Jim and Tracy did their own cooking. We don't know just when, but at some time they started having their evening meal every night with the Gibsons. Since Mrs. Gibson carried on a correspondence with Jim's mother, we may assume that Jim's mother, worried about Jim's health, paid the Gibsons for his board. The Gibson daughter, Inez, later said that the Gibson children adored Jim, who joked and played with them and taught them Harvard songs, perhaps off key.

Inez also told about how Jim would wash on the back porch before coming in to eat. He was very fond of floating island pudding, so her mother made it often for him. One night he mistook a pan of pudding which was cooling on the porch for the pan of wash water and sloshed it all over his face, much to the amusement of the children.

After Jim moved to Wahiawa, he and Tracy planted many different kinds of fruit and trees, such as watermelons, rose apples, star fruit, oranges, lemons, apples, peaches, pears, avocados, limes, grapes, coffee, cashew nuts, bananas, potatoes, etc. He had a eucalyptus tree in a tin can next to the kitchen and forgot about it. It grew and grew over the years and finally pushed in the walls of the kitchen. He also planted an elephant ear tree that grew to be one of the largest trees of its kind in Hawaii.

Jim and Tracy also began to plant pineapples. Their first attempt to grow pineapples, however, was not successful. Professor Storer had taught Jim that "if the soil is acid, lime it." The Wahiawa soil was acid, so Jim and Tracy limed one of their fields. Much to their dismay, they never grew a single pineapple in that field.

They had better success in other unlimed fields, so that, as Jim wrote later, "After some experimentation, I concluded that the land was better adapted to pineapples than to peas, pigs or potatoes, and accordingly concentrated on that fruit." After planting a few acres of pineapples, they then found themselves running around Honolulu peddling the pineapples.

Jim's parents in New England were pleased that he was now actively employed in some enterprise. The family and guests back in Boston toasted glasses of cider at Thanksgiving for the pineapple growers when the first crop was harvested, and his mother was delighted with the "wonderful pineapple pickles" that Mrs. Gibson sent her.

"The Excellent Fruit"

Historians agree that pineapple or "Ananus" (meaning "excellent fruit" in the language of the Guarani Indians of Paraguay from which the scientific name "Ananas comosus" is derived,) originated in Paraguay or Brazil. Pineapples are not generally grown from seeds, as such, but from the leafy crowns of the pineapples, the slips borne on the fruit stems or the suckers grown laterally from the fruit stems. Since all of these could still grow after being left unplanted for months, it is a plant that could easily be spread by ship from one place to another.

Pineapples were found in the Philippines before the arrival of the Spanish, and the fibers were used for clothing. In the 1500s and 1600s, pineapples were found growing in India, China, Africa, Australia, Mexico and other places.

After Columbus took pineapples home from the New World, people began to grow them in European greenhouses and they became a gourmet fruit in Europe. One account claims that a single pineapple sold in an auction in France for the equivalent of $50. With each fruit topped with a crown and with its good flavor, the pineapple was known as "the king of fruits." In Colonial New England, the pineapple became the symbol of hospitality, and pineapple shapes were carved on doorposts.

Pineapple, "halakahiki" in Hawaiian, meaning foreign fruit, had been growing in the Territory long before the Wahiawa homesteaders arrived. Wild pineapple, later to be known as the "Wild Kailua" variety of pineapple was found growing in the Kona area as early as 1816, indicating that the early Hawaiians probably had it. The early Polynesians evidently had pineapples in the

Marquesas. In the 1850s, pineapple was grown on most of the Islands.

It takes about eighteen months to two years to grow a pineapple from a crown, but, if it can avoid parasites, the plant may live for as long as fifty years. It must be grown in frost-free areas such as the tropics and sub-tropics, but it can grow with wide variations of water, in areas which may be as low as twenty inches of rain per year or in areas with considerable rainfall. The root system consists of a few long roots, which absorb water from the soil, and a mass of short roots around the stem, which absorb water overflowing from the leaf base. The plants may also absorb water from the atmosphere and store it in their leaves.

The first attempt to commercialize pineapples in Hawaii was in the early 1850s when some 21,000 pineapples of the Wild Kailua variety were shipped from Lahaina, Maui, to California to feed the gold rush miners.

While there are a number of varieties of pineapple, including the Wild Kailua, the Ripley Queen, the Sugar Loaf, Bahama, Mexican, Trinidad, among others, the Smooth Cayenne, introduced commercially to Hawaii in 1882 by horticulturalist Capt. John Kidwell became the most popular in Hawaii and elsewhere in the world. The Smooth Cayenne proved later to be ideal for canning because of its cylindrical form, uniform texture, and freedom from internal cavities, which meant easy handling and minimum waste.

Kidwell was an English sea captain who first saw the Smooth Cayenne variety of pineapples growing in hot-houses in England. He retired from the sea and became a dealer in exotic plants in San Francisco, then moved to Hawaii in 1882 to start a nursery in Manoa Valley, near Honolulu. A man named Lycan had picked up Smooth Cayenne pineapples from one of the early immigrant ships from the Azores, and had planted them in the Kalihi area of Honolulu. When he gave up on them, he sold his 300 plants to Kidwell. Kidwell grew them in Apokea in the Ewa district of Oahu.

E. W. Jordan, a contemporary of Kidwell, who first arrived in Hawaii in 1868 from England, grew and sold the Smooth Cayenne variety of pineapple in Hawaii in 1893 or 1894 after his brother, R. Jordan, shipped him 300 sets of them from Queensland, Australia. Jordan sold fresh pineapples in Honolulu for $1.00 each and also individual plants at $.25 each. Jordan and S.M. Damon then formed a partnership and began to experiment with growing them on a commercial scale in Moanalua, near Honolulu.

By the time Jim started growing pineapples, a number of the homesteaders were already in the business. Clark was the first. Kidwell had decided to convert his land to sugar rather than pineapple and dumped his pineapple stumps into ditches. Clark picked up the discarded pineapple stumps, planted them, and harvested his first crop in Wahiawa in 1900. The other Wahiawa growers also started planting pineapple because their vegetable crops were too difficult to sell. Their pineapples grew well, with some weighing as much as fifteen pounds.

Jim and the others at Wahiawa grew their pineapples primarily for the fresh market, but the market for fresh pineapples was limited in Hawaii. Fresh Hawaiian pineapple could not be shipped as far as the East Coast, but some pineapples were picked green and shipped to the West Coast. To do so was not very profitable, however, because the main summer crop of Hawaiian pineapples arrived in California at the same time that peaches, pears and other California fruit flooded the market. Jim began to think that the answer to producing pineapples profitably lay in canning them.

CANNING

Early slicing machine

The food canning industry was one of the new and high-tech industries of the day. The process of canning was originally developed by Nicholas Appert when he was trying to develop portable food to aid Napoleon's invasion of Russia. He developed the process of sealing peas in champagne bottles and then cooking them in water. He is generally considered to be the "founder of canning." His book, "The Art of Preserving all Vegetable Substances," was written in France in 1807.

The canning concept was later taken from France to England. Commercial canning was introduced into the U.S. in 1819 by William Underwood, who built the first American cannery in Boston. He canned a number of food products, one of which was "Underwood Deviled Ham."

During the 1820s, there were important fruit canners in Baltimore. Thomas Kensett and his father-in-law, Ezra Daggett, started canning a winter crop of white oysters in the Maryland city and a summer crop of fruits and vegetables. Later on, they started canning more exotic fruits and vegetables, including imports from South America. William Numsen canned fruit in Baltimore in the 1820s, and started canning pineapple there in the 1840s, which was spurred by trade between Baltimore and South America, exchanging grain, flower and corn meal from the U.S. for coffee and fruit.

The first big market for canned fruit outside of the East Coast was in California during the Gold Rush. So many people moved to California to mine gold with no intention of farming, that a ready market for canned goods developed. They would pay whatever the cost was for portable food. The California gold rush made Walter Baker Chocolates famous. The California miners bought all sorts of canned goods from Baltimore packers, including oysters, peaches, pineapple, chocolates, etc.

Increased demand for processed foods led to new canning technology. During this period, Isaac Solomon, who wanted to build a big oyster canning business in the Chesapeake Bay area, discovered that calcium chloride could be added to water which raised the temperature in the canning process and reduced the time of cooking. Unfortunately, calcium chloride salt corroded the cans, and when the cans were cooked with the calcium chloride, they swelled and exploded.

In 1874, a Baltimore canner by the name of Andrew Shriver, developed a retort kettle (a big pressure cooker) to heat canned goods under pressure, which eliminated the salt corrosion and the problem of cans exploding under heat. Stacks of canned goods could be put in it and heated under pressure without a salt bath. By being pressurized, the cans didn't swell and explode. This was a major technological breakthrough.

In 1881, a man by the name of Cox developed "The Cox Capper," a device which automated capping, the closure of the cans, and solved another "bottleneck" in mass canning.

With the retort kettle and the Cox Capper, the canning process could now be fully automated. Large amounts of pre-canned foods could be dumped into one end, canned, and capped on the other.

At first, the canning industry with all its manufacturing equipment was located in the city of Baltimore and used immigrant labor. In the 1800s the immigrant factory workers began to organize and strike. The first cannery strike in Baltimore was in 1872, with a larger and more difficult strike in 1874. After the Civil War, the newly freed slaves, who worked in the fields, were cheaper than immigrant labor, so some canneries moved out to the fields where the vegetables grew and used the freed slaves in the canneries. The canned goods were then shipped to Baltimore for export.

The early food canners in America included Heinz (1869), Campbell (1869), Stokley-Van Camp (1891), and many others who went out of business. The California fruit packing industry started in the late 1800s. Among the California pioneers was Hunt Bros.

American wars were a great stimulus for the canning industry. The Civil War was the first time an army relied extensively on military contracts for canned foods. The Spanish American War was another.

The first to commercially can pineapple in Hawaii were Ackerman and Muller in 1882. They peeled the pineapples, made cans by hand, and canned the pineapple on a kitchen stove, but they were unable to produce and ship their pineapple to the mainland in sufficient quantities to make a market.

Clark was the first to start canning pineapples in Wahiawa. His first cannery was the kitchen in his house, where he bottled pineapple in glass jars.

Kidwell also tried his hand at canning before he gave up on pineapples. With L.A. Thurston and John Emmeluth, he formed the Hawaiian Fruit & Packing Co., Ltd. in October, 1892. Most of the company's sales consisted of fresh pineapple for the local Hawaii market, but they also preserved pineapples, first in jars and later in tin cans. Their first pack of 486 cases of two dozen jars each was sold in 1895, some of the canned pineapple in California. While in operation, the company produced 400,000 fresh pineapples and 14,000 cases of canned pineapple.

But the business was unprofitable. A key problem was that all the cans had to be made by hand and it was difficult to get any economies of scale with quantity. Another problem was that, although there was no tariff on fresh fruit, there was a 35% U.S. tariff on processed food products shipped from Hawaii to the U.S. mainland.

In 1898, Kidwell leased his land to Ewa Plantation to grow sugar cane and sold his cannery to the Pearl City Fruit Company, who moved it into the hills above Pearl City. As it turned out, 1898 was the year the tariff on canned pineapple was lifted.

JIM STARTS HIS PINEAPPLE COMPANY

Once Jim started growing pineapple on his Wahiawa plantation, he realized that the market possibilities were huge in the United States and the rest of the world, if only he could "..extend the marketing season throughout the entire year..." Canning would do it and canning, he decided, was the only logical way to market Hawaiian pineapple. However, marketing on such a scale would require a cannery, and capital.

Jim's first attempts to finance his pineapple canning venture in 1901 were discouraging, as are most untried businesses, for investors generally prefer investing in proven enterprises. If Kidwell, the most seasoned in the field of commercial pineapple production quit, how could Jim expect to succeed? Why should one risk his money on a failure?

An editorial in the Honolulu Commercial Advertiser newspaper summed it up by referring to the prospects as "a foolhardy venture which had been tried unsuccessfully before and was certain to fail again." Another Advertiser editorial reasoned: "If pineapple paid, the vacant lots near town would be covered with them." Besides, capital was not readily available in Hawaii. Even Sanford wouldn't put his money into Jim's venture.

Undaunted by the opposition, the stubborn New Englander proceeded to canvass Honolulu, trying to encourage purchases of stock in the pineapple company he was about to start.

The Right Fruit

One early candidate was the Dowsett Company in Wahiawa. Dowsett was a major landowner in the area, owning some 20,000 acres adjacent to the Wahiawa Colony. Jim had met the manager, Walter Dillingham, in Boston before he had moved to Hawaii. Hopeful about Dowsett Company support, Jim waited for its decision before pursuing other sources of funds. Dillingham was interested but Dowsett was not.

Next, Jim contacted the attorney, Albert Francis Judd, Jr. to whom he had been given introduction in Boston, and this introduction proved to be a valuable one. The grandson of Dr. Garrett F. Judd, Jr., a medical missionary to Hawaii, and son of Albert Francis Judd, who had been Chief Justice of the Kingdom of Hawaii and Chief Justice of the Territorial Court, Albert Francis Judd, Jr. was a graduate of Yale law school, a trustee of Kamehameha and Punahou schools, the Bishop Museum and Bishop Trust, and was a corporate attorney, specializing in land matters.

Judd, just three years older than Jim, liked the idea of pineapple, but correctly felt that this was a major venture requiring extensive outside capital. He suggested that Jim "try to float the company in Honolulu," and said that he would be willing to incorporate the business and serve as the first president in exchange for stock. For him to be associated with the company would give it credibility and help its reputation. Jim accepted Judd's offer, and Judd drew up the articles of incorporation, was paid in stock, and became the first president of the company.

Hawaiian Pineapple Company, Limited (Hapco) was incorporated on December 4, 1901 with 1,000 shares of $20 par value common stock, of which 812 shares were subscribed, resulting in a total capitalization of $16,240.

To raise the initial capital for Hapco was no small undertaking. Based on a cost of living index developed by the Bank of Hawaii, the initial capital cost of the new company would be 14.33 times the 1901 cost, meaning that the $16,240 that Jim thought he needed to get the company off the ground would cost nearly $250,000 in 1988.

Jim, himself, subscribed for 200 shares of the stock, worth $4,000 at $20 each in exchange for the pineapple plants that were growing on his 61 acres at Wahiawa, a note guaranteeing the delivery of more within a year, a team of horses that he had previously purchased from the Dowsett Ranch, and a lease on 40 of the 61 acres that he owned, including the 10 acres on which the pineapple plants were growing.

Even without a cannery, money was needed to grow the pineapples, so Jim and Fred Tracy pooled their funds to advance Hapco $5,340 to cover the firm's working capital requirements. Jim raised his share of the advance by borrowing from relatives. His grandmother, Caroline Fletcher Dole, loaned him $1,000, with 6 percent interest, payable quarterly. His sister , Winifred, and his father loaned him $500 each, also at 6 percent, payable quarterly. This loan to the company was later cancelled in exchange for 267 shares of stock in order to get rid of the liability on the company's balance sheet, which might discourage new subscribers. These 267 additional shares of stock were held by Jim and Fred, with Jim as trustee.

Now Jim owned 200 shares outright and another 267 as trustee, indicating that he originally controlled 467 shares,

Giant elephant ear tree on the Wahiawa plantation

CHAPTER SEVEN

or 60 percent of the outstanding stock, which gave him majority control. No other single stockholder held more than 50 shares. Charles S. Dole, a second cousin, owned 25 shares. William R. Castle, Jr., Albert F. Judd, T. J. King, T. H. Gibson, and A. W. Eames, owned 50 shares each. Other stockholders and their respective subscriptions included Edgar Wood, 25; A. B. Ingalls, 10; Edward F. Boyd, 5; and Charles P. Grimwood, 5. The original stockholders were a diverse group:

Albert Judd, Jr. and A. L. C. Atkinson were law partners and were instrumental in incorporating the new company.

William R. Castle, Jr. was the son of Honolulu attorney and Castle & Cooke director, William Castle. He later became Ambassador to Japan and Undersecretary of State in the Hoover administration.

Thomas H. Gibson was the superintendent of the Boy's Industrial School, and later became Superintendent of Schools. Gibson was a Wahiawa planter, and Jim's neighbor and close friend.

E. P. F. (Eddie) Boyd was the Territorial Commissioner of Public Lands.

Charles P. Grimwood received five shares for handling the surveying of the 40 acres the company leased from Jim Dole.

Alfred W. Eames was a Wahiawa planter, who later sold his stock to start a competitive cannery in Wahiawa. His company was later acquired by the California Packing Corporation (CPC), which became Del Monte. His son, Alfred, became president of CPC.

Charles Sumner Dole was Jim Dole's second cousin, a son of Sanford's brother, George Dole. C.S. Dole was an attorney on Kauai and an avid polo player. He was subsequently thrown from his horse playing polo, landed on his head, and after being in a coma for weeks, lost his memory and was forced to give up his legal practice.

T. J. King was the owner of the California Feed Company, and took 50 shares in exchange for feed.

The original officers and directors were Albert F. Judd, president; T.J. King, vice president; T.H. Gibson, secretary; and Charles P. Grimwood, treasurer. All of the above officers were also directors. Walter F. Dillingham was the company's only non-officer director. Soon after incorporation and his surveying project, Grimwood resigned as treasurer and was replaced by Charles S. Dole. Jim Dole was made manager, and Fred Tracy, his assistant.

JIM GOES TO THE U.S. TO RAISE MORE MONEY

Field workers in the early days of pineapple

By the time a meeting of the stockholders was held on July 17, 1902, Jim and the other founders realized that it would cost much more than $16,240 to go into the canning business. In spite of the fact that all the initial $20,000 of stock wasn't fully subscribed, the stockholders approved increasing the number of shares by 1,250 which more than doubled the authorized stock of the corporation and increased the capitalization from $20,000 to $45,000. Also, in order to keep the new company afloat, the existing stockholders were to be assessed at the rate of 2-1/2 percent per month on each share.

Now Jim set out for Boston to try to sell more stock and raise $28,000, and he was away for a year while Tracy managed the plantation in Wahiawa. He went first to Boston, where he had a prospectus printed which outlined Hapco's resources and prospective plans, paying for the printing costs with one share of stock.

Unfortunately, the 1902 Hapco prospectus was lost sometime over the ensuing years, although excerpts of it have appeared in various sources. Only a couple of pages of his projections remain, in which a rough business plan was outlined. There is available, however, an article written by Jim, called "Pineapples," which draws a comparison between Hawaii and Florida pineapples at the time.

He put the cost of canning and other equipment at $7,100 and the annual payroll cost at $4,728: $900 to the manager (Dole), $600 to the teamster,

CHAPTER EIGHT

$600 to a processor for four months, $750 to a canner for five months, $998 to three Chinese men for fifteen months, and $880 to ten Chinese men for four months.

He estimated that, assuming the pineapple would be grown on company leased land with no outside purchase of pineapples, the growing cost of pineapples would be $50 per acre. (Later he increased it to $70 per acre.) With each acre producing 7.2 tons of fruit, his ten acres would produce 72 tons of fruit at an estimated cost per ton of $6.94 ($.00347 a pound). From his 72 tons of fruit, he expected to produce 7,062 cases of pineapple to be sold at a price of $3.00 per case of 24 cans, to be retailed at 35 cents a can. Taking all the costs into consideration, including shipping, he expected a profit of $.42 per case. This would result in a profit of $2,966 for the first year.

With only ten acres in production, the projections sounded good. After the cannery was in place and more pineapples canned, the profit would rise. Even if no cans of pineapple were sold the first year, with capital stock of $45,000 Jim thought the firm would have $4,000 available after the first year.

One of the most important points Jim could make in selling his idea was that, since the annexation of Hawaii to the United States in 1898, there no longer were duties on pineapple imported into the U.S. Without the added cost of the tariff, Hawaiian pineapples were now at an advantage. The 35 percent tariff on canned pineapple made it impractical to can it in a foreign location. There was also a duty of $.0175 per lb. on pineapples shipped in green from the Bahamas and the West Indies and canned in Baltimore. Without the duty on pineapples, a tremendous American market had been opened up for canned pineapples. Earlier attempts to can pineapple had not been successful because of the lack of this U.S. market. "The preserving of pineapple in cans... now promises to become a leading industry of the new Territory. It extends the market for Hawaiian pineapples into every grocery store in the United States."

A point Jim made in his article, "Pineapples," was that it was cheaper to raise pineapples in Hawaii than in Florida. He cited the "Farmer's Bulletin No. 140. U.S. Department of Agriculture, 1901" which put land costs in Florida between $80-$150 per acre. Added to raw land costs were costs associated with clearing, plants, fertilizer, labor and shedding. Total costs of land and improvements in Florida ranged from $417 to $1,765 per acre, excluding the manager's salary. In Hawaii there was little expense for clearing land, because only the "wild grass" had to be removed by burning. There were no shedding costs for Hawaiian pineapple as there were in Florida as the temperatures were more moderate in Hawaii. Also, there was no requirement for fertilizer for at least the first couple of ratoons, as the soil was rich. Labor was lower, too, in Hawaii than in Florida.

Jim also made the point that, although pineapples were being canned in other parts of the world, canned Hawaiian pineapples were superior. The fruit from Florida was "...tough, sour, and with very little pineapple flavor..."

Later articles spoke of the superiority of Hawaiian pineapples. An article in the June 18, 1903 edition of the Pacific Commercial Advertiser said that Sumatra and Singapore pines were of an inferior grade, and that the pineapples grown in the Bermudas and Florida did not have the flavor of the Hawaiian fruit because they had to be picked green before being sent to Baltimore to be canned. The Hawaiian pineapples had a better flavor because they could be allowed to ripen before being picked and then canned immediately.

Returning from the mainland

An article by Wells Goodhue of Chicago in the May 17, 1904 Pacific Commercial Advertiser said that canners in Baltimore had only been able to make $0.025 per can on canned pineapple because of slow demand, even with a price to the wholesaler of $3.00 per case. It speculated that the higher quality Hawaiian pineapple could retail for $1.00 per can. (Compared with Jim Dole's recommended list price of $0.35 per can.)

Full of enthusiasm for his plan, Jim, with the aid of Harvard classmate and stock promoter, Philip Melancthon Tucker, sold 385 shares in Boston, raising $7,700. Subscriptions in amounts ranging between five and a hundred shares were sold to fifteen individual stockholders. Stockholders included a number of Harvard "Class of 1899" classmates, including Charles Perkins

Adams, 25 shares; John Easton Rousmaniere, 5 shares; and Horace Dudley Hall Williams, 10 shares. Family friends included Edward and Helen S. Brewer, who together bought 125 shares. Happy that he attracted any investors at all, Jim was still far short of his goal.

One of the Boston stockholders was classmate John Rousmaniere, who, after law school, joined the Boston law firm, Matthews, Thompson & Spring. He looked at the Hapco investment as a "flyer" but remained a faithful stockholder throughout Hapco's early growth years. His sister, F. Rousmaniere, later bought stock.

Once the stock was sold, Tucker, who had recently joined Barnard & Gibson Investment Securities, took on the responsibility of monitoring Hapco stock for the Boston investors, and continued to do so later when he started his own investment firm.

During the summer Jim was on the East coast, he made a trip to Southwest Harbor and talked his friend John Whitmore, who was working for a sardine cannery, into coming to Hawaii to join him in his pineapple venture.

Just before Jim left Boston, his cousin Sanford Ballard Dole visited Jim's family in Jamaica Plain. When Sanford left for Washington, Jim traveled with him. On the way, Sanford talked about his concern over the possibility of snakes entering the Territory. Prior to the U.S. annexation of Hawaii, the laws of the Kingdom and Republic of Hawaii prevented the entry of snakes, but, after the annexation, there were no such laws for the Territory. Sanford asked Jim to try to get the same provision into the laws of the Territory and gave him a letter of introduction to Secretary Wilson, the Secretary of Agriculture.

After they arrived in Washington, Jim went on to Baltimore, the capital of the American canning industry, where he bought pineapple slicing equipment from the George W. Zastrow Company with part of the money he had been able to raise.

While in the East, Jim also bought $5,500 worth of canning equipment. Purchased were a boiler and engine from the Erie City Iron Works,, and peelers from E. J. Lewis in Middlebrook, New York.

After Baltimore, Jim went back to Washington to call on Secretary Wilson. After a considerable wait, he entered the Secretary's office to plead his case. He said that soldiers returning from the Spanish-American War in the Philippines were bringing their pet snakes into Hawaii, using them to catch rats. Wilson took off his spectacles and said: "Are you trying to be a St. Patrick of Hawaii?" Nevertheless, Jim was able to impress on him the urgency of the situation, and Secretary Wilson promised to discuss the matter with his cabinet. To this day, snakes have been banned from Hawaii.

Jim must have been disappointed not to have sold more stock in Boston, but undaunted he continued on his way. After Washington, he headed for San Francisco to see Samuel Sussman, president of Sussman, Wormser and Company (S&W) to whom he had a letter of introduction from Charles Grimwood.

Sussman, Wormser and Company, S&W Fine Foods today, was formed in 1896 as a San Francisco, California wholesale grocery distributor. The three founders were Samuel Sussman, Gustav Wormser and Samuel I. Wormser. The Wormsers were first cousins, and Sussman was the brother-in-law of Gustav. Jacob (Jake) Blumlein, a nephew of the

Wormsers, was general manager and canned goods buyer. The business originally had seventeen employees and six sales representatives making deliveries in one-horse buggies, and the main warehouse was located on the corner of Fremont and Market Streets in San Francisco. S&W started at a time when the canning industry was in its infancy in California. At that time, the California canning industry consisted of a number of small, privately owned firms. There was a considerable variation of quality in the canned foods of the various canners. S&W, which marketed canned food products under the S&W label, rejected products that failed to meet its standards.

Jake Blumlein had already become interested in canned pineapple after he had been successful in marketing a shipment of pineapple packed by the Hawaiian Fruit & Packing Company. While Jim had been back East raising money, Jake was in Hawaii studying the possibility of building a cannery. He surveyed the new pineapple plantations in the Territory, and towards the end of the year returned to Hawaii with the intention of erecting a cannery. The project proved more expensive than he anticipated and when he ran out of money, he gave up on it.

Jim met Samuel Sussman and Jake Blumlein in San Francisco, and discussed selling stock to them. As Jim wrote later, "Mr. Sussman, on first acquaintance, was somewhat awe inspiring. I didn't sell him." Also, if Sussman bought a large block of stock, he wanted a discount. Jim said he couldn't give him stock at a lower price, because it would be unfair to the other stockholders. Blumlein was eager to do a deal, but Sussman balked.

Jim then went back to Hawaii, discouraged. He had not only failed to raise the money he needed, but had bought machinery he might not be able to use.

OFF TO A SHAKY START

Jim's Wahiawa home, after considerable expansion

Then Sussman changed his mind. As it happened, he was impressed with Jim and gained confidence in him when he refused to sell him stock at a lower price. Perhaps Jake Blumlein also helped talk him into it. At any rate, on December 11, 1902, Samuel Sussman offered to take 500 shares of Hapco stock on the condition that his company would have the exclusive rights to distribute all of Hapco's pineapple production and to receive a 5 percent agency commission for its services.

The offer for the stock alone would have raised 40 percent of the capital which was so badly needed, but nevertheless Jim and the Hapco board did not like the idea of Hapco being stuck with only one distributor and insisted that Sussman and/or S&W be given distribution rights only for the West Coast of the U.S., that the agency arrangement

be renewed annually and that it could be terminated with a six months notice. Sussman did not like the terms and backed out.

From the beginning, Sussman hadn't wanted to get involved unless an experienced canner was with Hapco. He suggested to Joseph Hunt of Santa Rosa, founder of Hunt Brothers Packing Company (Hunt Bros.– the Producer of Hunt's Ketchup) that he visit Hapco in Wahiawa.

Hunt Bros. was one of the earlier California fruit canners whose products were distributed by S&W. Hunt Bros. had been started in 1890 by Joseph and William Hancock Hunt, two brothers who helped their mother can fruits and vegetables each summer when they were growing up. When their mother died in 1888, they decided to open a small canning business on the family ranch in

Santa Rosa. They incorporated in 1890 as Hunt Brothers' Fruit Packing Company and constructed a cannery in Santa Rosa, California. Their first pack was 30,000 cases of fruits and vegetables. In order to get closer to their main sources of fruit supply in the San Joaquin Valley, they soon moved the cannery to Hayward, California. William Hunt died in 1896 and Joseph continued the business alone.

Joseph Hunt did visit Hawaii, and was immediately enthusiastic about the prospects of pineapple canning there. The very afternoon Hunt arrived in Honolulu, Jim took him out to Wahiawa by horse and buggy, pulled by Withers and Charley, to inspect the plantation. It took five hours to get there, just enough time for the exuberant New Englander to fully sell Hunt on the possibilities of his prospective new company. Hunt's partner, A. C. Baumgartner, was also impressed with the company. Jim later said of Hunt that he was "one of the most successful canners of California, and proprietor of what is probably the second largest fruit cannery in the world."

The company was in rather a desperate state, so when Hunt wanted to make a deal to sell their pineapples, Hapco was not as demanding this time, and entered into an agency arrangement with Hunt on April 4, 1903 which made Hunt Brothers the sole agent to distribute Hapco's entire output of canned pineapple anywhere for a commission of 5 percent on gross sales. The contract with Hunt was an exclusive five year arrangement, which stipulated that Hunt would collect all funds from the sale of canned pineapples and only remit to Hapco the residual balance after its commissions were deducted. Pineapple could be sold both under Hunt's and Hapco's own labels. In addition to the agency arrangement, Hunt Bros. agreed to arrange for Hapco the supply of cans from

American Can Company, its own supplier. Hunt soon thereafter sent over one of his accountants, Archie W. Adams, to be Hapco's bookkeeper.

Jim later attributed much of the early success of the company to Hunt: "We are very fortunate in having Hunt Bros. Co. as our sales agent. Its activity in introducing and placing our goods has built us up a splendid trade and I feel that this, together with our facilities for turning out our product at much less cost than most of the Island producers puts us in an impregnable position as to competition."

S&W was not completely out of the picture. Hunt would take a commission on all canned pineapple he sold, while S&W would actually do the distributing of the pineapple cases. All the pieces were being put in place.

It was after Hunt got involved in 1903 that Jim was able to proceed on his dream of building "the largest and most complete pineapple cannery in the world, as soon as production justifies it."

Meanwhile, the pace of the developing business was a little too fast for Fred Tracy. He liked it better in the old days when he and Jim were peddling fresh pineapples on the street. Besides, he started dating Miss Bevin, a school teacher in Wahiawa in early 1903, and married her not long after.

Jim and Tracy had entwined their finances, which now caused a problem. Jim's father scolded Jim in a letter written on July 13, 1903, for having his finances intermingled with Fred Tracy's, but a few days later on July 18, 1903, he sent Jim $500 as a 4 percent loan to help him free himself from the arrangement. Tracy and his new bride left Hawaii and he took a job at a ranch in Grangerville, Idaho. They later moved to Alaska where Fred was employed as a hydraulic mine operator for several years. They returned to Hawaii, and Fred became a foreman at the Thomas Pineapple Company, until

Fred Tracy, Jim, Inez and Maile Gibson

moving to Kauai, where he worked as a ditch luna (foreman), a carpenter, and a handyman on one of the sugar plantations. He died on Kauai in 1925 or 1930 from liver cancer, which Jim jokingly attributed to his cooking while they homesteaded in Wahiawa.

Jim continued to manage the plantation without Tracy but with the help of Ah Wo, a young Chinese man. Ah Wo remained a faithful employee at Wahiawa for the rest of his life. He not only helped with the field work but did the cooking. He later married, raised a family, and his children became upstanding members of the community.

Luckily, between July, 1902 and June, 1903, the pineapple company was able, with more than a dozen new stockholders, to raise an additional $13,000 of capital. In less than two years Jim had been able to sell 1,873 shares and raise $37,460, nearly 85 percent of his goal.

Before long, Hapco began building its cannery. It bought a commercial site from Carol Pullman, a Wahaiwa homesteader, to construct a 3,900 square foot cannery. Adjacent to the cannery, the

firm put up a barn large enough for six horses and laborer's quarters for up to twelve workers. When finished, the cannery and all its associated equipment cost $13,100, well above the $7,100 estimated in the 1902 prospectus.

The cannery was a 3,900 square-foot wood frame building with crude hand operated equipment. Packers stuffed pineapple slices into cans through small holes in the tops and then soldered them shut. Sometimes solder dripped into the cans.

Hapco bought all its original cans from the American Can Company's factory in San Francisco, the company which made the cans for Hunt's cannery. Hapco used about 43,000 cans in 1903. The figure jumped to 600,000 in 1905, and to 900,000 in 1906.

The first cans blew up by the thousands, some in the dealers' warehouses. About 25 percent of the 1906 pack was lost. This problem was solved eventually by sealing machines, which mechanically placed a cover on each can. The cover was larger than the top of the can, so its edge was crimped under and rolled over without solder, and only the seams were soldered. This process also avoided solder drops in the pineapple cans. Once the cans were properly sealed, they were deposited into one end of giant cookers which sterilized them, and cooked them and then discharged them out the other end.

The company also kept increasing its acreage and planting more pineapples. In July, 1902, Hapco was leasing 40 acres from Jim, of which 10 were planted, and the company had an option to lease another 300 acres from the Dowsett Company, thanks to Walter Dillingham, the manager. A year later, about 30 acres were planted, and another 50 acres were leased from the Dowsett Company which were cleared and made ready for planting. An agreement with Dowsett was also reached to lease several hundred acres of additional land in the adjoining area which Hapco would sublease to farmers rent-free if they would grow pineapple on the land and sell it to the Hapco cannery.

The new plantings for the additional acres were partially from lateral suckers originating from the original plant crop which were replanted in the company's nursery, and by outside purchases. 92,000 plants were bought from E. W. Jordan for cash plus $2,100 worth of Hapco stock. Including the plants bought from Jordan, Hapco now had a total of 145,000 pineapple plants and 125,000 shoots.

But other problems were beginning to develop. Not only were costs higher than expected but the number of cases

Hapco's Wahiawa cannery

packed was lower. Jim found that it was costing him nearly twice as much as expected to get started. Nor were there as many pineapples produced as he had projected. Because of drainage problems and poor soil conditions, the 1903 crop of pineapples was estimated to total 35,000 pineapples, which would mean that the company would harvest only 70 tons from its own crop. With 50 or more tons purchased from other Wahiawa growers, Hapco would be processing 120 tons during its first canning season, which was a pack amounting to only 1,893 cases, well below the estimate of over 7,000.

In his report to directors and stockholders in June 1903, Jim said that, even assuming cash revenues of $10,000 in the 1903 year, Hapco would need an additional $20,000 to carry it through the 1904 pack, or it would go out of business. Enough cash had been raised from the sale of stock to buy equipment and go into the business of processing pineapple, but there was not sufficient cash to operate. At the end of June, 1903, the Board agreed to increase monthly assessments of stockholders from 2-1/2 percent to 10 percent per month.

By September, 1903, the pack was canned and shipped to Hunt, but it would take time before any cash would arrive from its sale, so the company again needed cash. This time it set out to borrow at least $4,000.

Now Hunt began to buy stock. He bought all the 377 remaining unsubscribed but unsold shares and 350 shares held by minority stockholders, over a third of the company stock, and became the single largest stockholder of Hapco, owning even more stock than Jim. From the new shares sold, the corporation received $7,540.

Among the sellers were some of the original founders of Hapco who were probably tired of the hassle and wanted their money back. Judd and Atkinson decided to go back to practicing law, resigned their positions, and sold their interests to Hunt. Gone were Jordan and Thomas Gibson. The only original officer was T. H. King. Walter Dillingham and John Whitmore both bought 50 and 15 shares, respectively and Whitmore was made a director. In November 1903 Jim Dole was elected president for the first time.

Phil Tucker tried to keep the Boston contingent of stockholders happy as long as he could, but a number wanted to sell and did so to Hunt through Jim. One of his letters to Jim said: "I have been to see a number of your stockholders and a few seem disposed to sell if they can, as they went in to help you." Others wanted to stick with it.

Horace D. H. Williams, who had bought 10 shares, was especially concerned because he was a close friend and a Harvard classmate. He was concerned that the number of cases which had been projected at 7,000 hadn't even reached 2,000. Jim offered to repurchase the shares, but Horace did not accept. He decided to hold on to his shares in hopes that the business would eventually get off the ground.

Col. Thomas L. Livermore, holder of 50 shares, just wondered where his dividend was.

Jim was shattered at the thought of disillusioning his family and friends and tried to reimburse them for their loss of income. There was no loss of capital because all transactions were conducted at the par value of $20 a share. All were impressed at Jim's sense of honor, and none would accept interest when he offered it. Charles Bowditch, who had loaned Jim the $2,000 to buy the Wahiawa land and had apparently exchanged this loan for Hapco stock, wrote from Boston on January 12, 1904, saying that a reimbursement of principal and interest on an equity investment was entirely unnecessary. He accepted the principal but not the interest and he returned a check sent him for the interest.

Another stockholder, Edward Brewer, who sold his shares, wrote on July 5, 1904, thanking Jim for proposing to reimburse him for the interest on his investment in Hapco stock and said, "I cannot admit however any liability on your part for such loss of interest. The profit which might have been made, would have been mine, however large, and the loss is for me a loss to bear." He thanked Jim for finding him a buyer for his stock.

Phil Tucker and the Boston investors who remained as investors became wary because Hunt controlled the company's source of cans and they thought he had deliberately held up the supply of cans in order to hurt the company so that he could buy more stock at depressed prices. It was true that it was only after the disappointing results of the 1903 pack was out that Hunt bought stock.

Phil wrote Jim, "Your holders rely on you to look out for their interests and don't want the company heavy borrowers, or involved too closely with men they don't know. The responsibility is yours but they have confidence you will act right." Phil thought that he could arrange for distribution of canned pineapple on the East Coast and that New England could soon easily absorb 20,000 cases of canned pineapple. He suggested that Jim sever his relationship with Hunt.

After discussing the matter with Jim's father, Phil's concerns toned down somewhat, and he wrote: "A businessman must pull together with his associates in order to do well, and suspicion tends to bring about the very thing we may suspect."

Phil felt that in order for the Boston group to influence the business, they had to be in control. At one point they did own 945 shares, including Jim's stock, Jim's mother's stock and other shares Phil placed subsequent to Jim's

trip to Boston, plus the 385 shares Jim originally sold while in Boston. This was more than Hunt owned at the time. If the Boston stockholders voted as a block, they could control the company. Phil encouraged Jim at this point to selectively place more stock through him in Boston for commission so that Hunt couldn't get more stock. Phil's concerns were grounded on the belief that Hunt would restrict dividend payments to stockholders if he were in control. As a strategy in selling more stock in the East, Tucker suggested that Jim put together a new prospectus with a business plan and go to the Boston backers through Phil for more equity capital.

Jim, perhaps spurred by Tucker's suspicions, was wary about Hunt's motives, but was calmed by his father. In a letter of April 30, 1903, his father lectured him about the importance of trusting others, for without trust, commerce suffers. His father went on to say: "If you venture you must trust as much as you can, for suspicion hurts such a relation as you have come into with these San Francisco people. I don't see why it is not to their advantage to have your service."

"I hold that pioneers are always entitled to their reward," Charles wrote further, "but if they set it too high, they doubtless provoke excessive competition. It must be difficult at first to know when the reward should be, since there are so many risks to be hazarded. But it seems to me that the main intent of the soundness of a business should be to provide as excellent and as large a product as may be, and that they cross the lines of justice when they begin to exert themselves to make their own profit paramount concern, as for example, to check and forbid the natural development of their kind of business in order to control the profit for themselves. It is fair to everyone that a legitimate business should attract other men into its development."

HAPCO GROWS

Selecting pineapple that offered the best quality

Before long Jim's prophecy that there would be a big demand for canned Hawaiian pineapples and that canning them would be profitable began to come true, and the pineapple industry grew rapidly from its inception in 1901 to become in 1915 Hawaii's second largest industry.

In 1901, when the Pearl City Fruit Co. produced 2,083 cases, people didn't know about pineapples and at first there was little or no demand, but later, when the price was reduced from around $2.00 a dozen cans to $1.25 a dozen, the pineapples went with a rush. "The wholesalers absorbed the whole lot, distributed them to the retailers, and at once there arose a demand. People who had been using pines from Sumatra and Singapore, immediately demanded the Hawaiian fruit, and since the wholesalers had made a big profit, they responded quickly with a demand for more," wrote

the Pacific Commercial Advertiser on June 18, 1903.

According to the same edition of the Pacific Commercial Advertiser, "The interest taken in Hawaiian pineapple has proven immense. Already three of the greatest houses in San Francisco have sent representatives to make an effort to secure the entire pack of the islands under contract. This has not been done, but some of the packers have indicated their willingness to enter into agreements for the sale of all their goods which are to be sent outside the Islands."

The article went on to speculate as to opportunities in various lines of pineapple preserves, such as pineapple sweet pickles, pineapple jam, pineapple marmalade, and pineapple syrup, among others. It also suggested that one of the greatest uses for canned pineapples might lie in saloons. "For punches and similar mixtures for hot weather consumption, the long slices across the pineapple are used, and so great has become the demand for this class of goods, that one of the local canneries will make its entire export pack of this shape."

Hapco's pack increased after its first frustrating year to 8,810 cases in 1904. But its problems were by no means over. The bulk of the pineapple crop was picked and canned between June 1st and November 30th. Working capital was needed to process the pineapples growing in the fields, to pick and can them, and to carry the company until it got paid from the sales of pineapple. Although Hapco's canned pineapple pack was 8,810 cases in 1904, it needed still more money.

Disgruntled with the Bank of Hawaii, the firm switched banking affiliations to Bishop & Co.(First Hawaiian Bank), which allowed bank overdrafts of up to $20,000 with interest, secured by the assets of Hapco and with personal guarantees from Samuel Sussman, Jacob Blumlein, Joseph Hunt, A. O. Baumgartner, and Jim Dole. The overdraft represented a demand note, meaning that the bank could call the money back at any time.

The guarantee of the bank overdraft represented the first time S&W had any direct financial relationship with Hapco, for neither the food distributor or its officers or directors owned any Hapco stock. However, both Hunt and Sussman granted Hapco a line of credit to borrow a sum not exceeding $5,000 from them for a period no longer than one year. The overdraft authority and the line of credit, gave Hapco a ready source of up to $25,000 to process its 1904 pineapple pack.

When the company wanted to expand the Wahiawa plantation, and to upgrade the cannery so that it could handle a larger pack, Hapco decided to raise new capital by selling additional

Woman field worker in unique clothing

stock. It was decided to double the outstanding common stock to $90,000, selling the new stock again at the par value of $20 per share. The stock was offered to the existing stockholders in proportion to the number of shares presently held. Over 40% of the stock at the end of 1904 was owned by Hunt, about half that by Jim. Only Jim and T. J. King were among the original stock holders left in the company.

Not all the new stock authorized was sold, but $28,000 that was issued was picked up by Hunt. Jim only added 105 shares. A number of the minority stockholders also sold out to Hunt. Most of the minority shareholders were now gone, including Dillingham and King, with the exception of a few of Jim's Harvard buddies and his mother. Hunt now clearly controlled the corporation, holding over 70 percent of all the outstanding stock. Jim owned only 16 percent. However, in spite of his majority position in Hapco, Hunt did not choose to be either an officer or director of the company.

Hunt gained control despite Tucker's efforts, and Phil acknowledged his defeat. When Frank Sweetzer of Boston wanted to sell his stock, he sold it to

Hunt. Tucker, along with a number of Boston stockholders, also wanted out, not so much because of the poor financial showing in 1903, but because Hunt was now in control and, in their opinion, would certainly restrict dividend payments to them. They thought that there was a definite conflict of interests with Hunt being both the key stockholder and the company's sole selling agent. Phil wrote Jim: "None of your friends here have lost any confidence in you and we all hope you'll come out all right yourself." Many of the Boston stockholders sold to Hunt for prices between $20 and $25 per share. Phil, however, changed his mind and held on to his shares, and later when Hapco doubled its capital stock from $45,000 to $90,000, Tucker asked for an additional four shares for himself.

Hapco continued to acquire more land and to plant more pineapples. Jim wanted to develop his business rapidly because he did not want to lose the financial backing of Hunt or Sussman, and he was worried about competition from the other Wahiawa planters, and from Puerto Rico, which, close to New York, was becoming a competitive threat.

In 1905, he wanted to lease 700 acres from the John Ii Estate, Ltd. for a twenty year duration, with an option of up to 1,500 acres, but Hunt held up the agreement because he objected to obligating the company to a long term lease of 20 years. Jim was so sure he was right in leasing the land that he made a personal offer to the Estate of $500 per annum in advance for a three year option on 1,500 acres to the end of 1907, and he offered to pay above market rents. He figured that if Hapco failed to follow through on the leases, he would have a claim on the land and would be able to exercise his option and sublease the land to other growers. No confirmation record was available, but apparently Jim's offer was accepted.

In a letter to Charles Brown, manager of the John Ii Estate, Jim told Brown that the company would be a secure tenant, because, with Hunt and Sussman's backing, Hapco was the only pineapple plantation in Wahiawa that would be financially capable of planting and marketing over 1,000 acres of pineapples grown on the Estate's land.

After acquiring the Ii Estate land, the company had 1,000 acres planted in pineapple. Not long after, the pineapple acreage was boosted again by leasing another 300 acres, bringing the total pineapple acreage of the company to 1,300 in 1908.

By Oct. 25, 1906, Hapco was able to complete its $45,000 financing, including an additional 721 shares to Hunt in March, and 50 shares to John Whitmore, 35 shares to Jim Dole and 12 shares to Frances Dole. Hunt essentially bought all the newly issued shares, and some more on the open market. As of October 25, 1906, Hunt owned a total of 3,300 shares of Hapco stock, or 73 percent of all the stock of the corporation. Jim Dole's interest now was down to 14 percent.

One of the things the company did with the proceeds of the new stock sale was to purchase 40 of Jim Dole's Wahiawa acres for $4,000 and to reimburse Hunt $1,000 for his trips back and forth between San Francisco and Hawaii. This land was later sold by the company as it decided to put its money into leasing land, rather than to tying up cash in land holdings. This strategy later proved to be a mistake, as many of the leases were for short terms.

Hapco's pack increased from 8,818 cases in 1904, to 25,022 cases in 1905, 31,934 cases in 1906, and 108,600 cases in 1907, with average operating profits of about $0.50 per case, which meant about $4,405 in 1904, $12,511 in 1905, $15,967 in 1906, and $54,300 in 1907.

THE CANNERY IS MOVED TO HONOLULU

Dillingham's Oahu Rail and Land Company transported fruit to the Honolulu cannery

When the Wahiawa cannery was built, and for the five years it was there, there was no railroad line to connect it with a major commercial area. The roads were merely wagon trails, and shipment of supplies from Honolulu was a one week roundtrip via mule team.

In 1906, the American Can Company agreed to build a can-making factory in Honolulu. Now it became obvious that it would be much better if the cannery were in town, close not only to its source of cans from the American Can Company, but to its shipping points and to the labor supply. The move became possible when Oahu Rail and Land Company (OR&L) agreed to link a railroad line between Wahiawa and Honolulu by a branch line between Waipahu and Wahiawa, so that fresh pineapples could still be picked ripe and immediately shipped to Honolulu to be canned.

It was a big advantage to the company to have a can-making plant next door. Not only would the cannery get the cans it needed, but it would not have to provide the warehouses to store them before using them, nor, if it made its own cans, spend the money for the can-making equipment needed or spend time and effort needed to keep up with new technological developments.

Hapco first planned to move to Honolulu in 1906, but the San Francisco fire prevented Hunt from paying Hapco for the cases he sold, so the move was postponed until 1907. The new cannery, along with two warehouses and an office building, was built on Iwilei Road next to the can plant. The Wahiawa cannery was demolished and its machinery moved into the new cannery.

To move the cannery to Honolulu required more money, so, at a meeting on August 5, 1907, the stockholders agreed to increase the capital stock from

$90,000 to $400,000, and the authorized stock to $500,000. The offer was made more attractive by providing at the same time a stock dividend for existing shareholders. A total of 15,500 new shares would be issued at $20.00 per share, of which 11,250 new shares would be issued as a 250 percent stock dividend, and the remaining 4,250 shares would be offered to existing shareholders as a rights offering based on shares currently held. Shares not subscribed would be sold on the open market through Halstead & Company, a Honolulu investment banker. This 1907 financing represented the first public offering of Hapco stock, which was to trade the next year at a range of $22 to $25 per share.

By June 16, 1908, after the distribution of the stock dividend, over 4,250 new shares were sold, which, at $20 a share, must have brought in $85,000 in new capital. This time, Hunt only bought a few shares, and while he still owned over 58 percent of all the stock, his percentage declined.

Of the unsubscribed shares, 600 were purchased by Hapco employees, and 2,150 shares were sold in the open market. This trend of employee ownership of Hapco continued while Jim Dole was president and chief executive officer.

At the same time, Jim's share of the stock decreased. He now only owned a few more shares than he owned back in 1903. He had owned 490 shares in 1903, 630 shares before the stock dividend, and 1,575 shares after the stock dividend. Then he sold 894 shares, leaving him with 681 shares, which reduced his percentage of the total outstanding stock to 3.4 percent. In 1908 or 1909, he scaled down his holdings by 50 shares to 631 shares.

By the 1907 financing, Hapco was a totally changed company. Fixed assets had increased from $13,000 to $160,000, while inventories had increased from $15,000 to $200,000. Banking needs to harvest the peak summer pack had increased from $20,000 to $200,000. Growth was well in place.

Boxing fruit for the cannery

CHAPTER ELEVEN

OTHER PINEAPPLE COMPANIES

Original C.P.C. Cannery in Wahiawa

Hapco wasn't the only pineapple canner. Some of the other pineapple growers in Wahiawa tried their hand early at canning pineapples. Will P. Thomas, who had supplied pineapple to Hapco, started the Thomas Pineapple Company, which included a cannery in the Kalihi district of Honolulu. In 1916, he sold out to Libby, McNeill & Libby of Honolulu, Ltd.

Libby was a Maine corporation, which had acquired the Ahuimanu Pineapple and Ranch Company, Ltd. on Oahu, including a controlling interest in a small Honolulu cannery. The company started leasing land on the windward side of Oahu and later expanded to the islands of Maui and Molokai. Libby became the second largest pineapple packer, next to Hapco.

Another Wahiawa pineapple grower, Alfred W. Eames, was Jim's neighbor and one of the original stockholders who had founded Hapco. After he recognized the potential of pineapple canning, he sold his Hapco stock and joined with Byron Clark, another of the Wahiawa pineapple growers, to form a competitive cannery in Wahiawa, the Tropic Fruit Company. Tropic Fruit was incorporated in September 1902, about a year after the incorporation of Hapco, with a capitalization of about $80,000. The first pack was in glass containers. In 1906, Tropic Fruit merged with a new company called Consolidated Pineapple Company of Wahiawa, which was a consolidation of Tropic Fruit and the Hawaiian Fruit and Plant Company. The consolidated company also did business under the name of Wahiawa Consolidated Company. Another pineapple pioneer in this corporation originally was Will Thomas. The combined company had a capitalization of about $200,000. Despite its financial backing, which included about $102,000 of advances from Castle & Cooke, the company had problems marketing its pineapple and liquidated its assets, selling out to Eames. Eames also bought the assets of the Hawaiian Islands Packing Company, which included Consolidated's Wahiawa cannery. When Eames retired, his son sold out to C.P.C. in 1917, but stayed with C.P.C. and later became its president.

California Packing Co. (C.P.C), was a California corporation born in the heart of a growing California fruit packing industry with its head office located in San Francisco. It was a huge California canner involved in the packing of peaches, other fruits, dried fruits, mackerel, sardines, tuna, salmon, vegetables, etc.. C.P.C. leased 4,315 acres of pineapple land in Wahiawa from Waialua Agriculture. (Later it acquired or leased other acreage on Oahu, on Molokai, and in the Philippines, where C.P.C.'s subsidiary, started in 1926, owned a cannery.) C.P.C. became the third largest pineapple company in Hawaii.

By 1907, the Hawaii growers had increased their output by four times. Hapco processed 3,000 tons of pineapple that year and packed 108,600 cases, which was 56 percent of the entire Hawaii pineapple pack. It had 2,100 acres planted and expected in 1908 to have a crop from 900 acres, process 4,704 tons and pack 225,320 cases. In 1908, 400,000 cases of pineapple were packed by the industry, with Hapco packing the most.

After the American Can factory was in place in Honolulu and fully operating in 1907, 2.4 million cans were used, and the figure kept going up. By 1930, the can plant was manufacturing 300 million cans for Hapco and the other canneries.

At first when there had not been much production of pineapples, and the demand was high, there was not much trouble selling the cans produced, but now, with Hapco and all the other companies producing more and more canned pineapple, it is not surprising that before long there were problems of overproduction.

The first time prices fell because of overproduction was in 1909. In 1907, the United States was hit by a depression, following the "Panic of 1907" that was brought on by a 50 percent drop in the price of copper in six months. The Knickerbocker Trust Company closed its doors and there was a run on the Trust Company of America. Many canneries on the mainland had to close down, and the Hawaiian pineapple canners, too, began to be affected.

Orders for pineapple were being cancelled. Jim commented in his 1908 Annual Report to Stockholders on June 16, 1908 that, "Our stock of pineapple would no doubt have been entirely cleaned up if it had not been for the depression which has followed the financial crisis in the United States."

In 1909 when the number of tons Hapco processed had increased 90 percent, with 242,822 cases packed, only 60,000 cases were sold on the futures market before the brunt of the depression was felt. Then, from spring 1908 to February 1909, when over 100,000 cases of pineapple were packed, 70 percent of the previous pack were still unsold, and only 10,000 more were sold.

Some people thought that this was the "beginning of the end" of canned pineapple. Jim saw it as "a time when something decides whether a business will be great or diminish."

THE INDUSTRY ADVERTISES

Early advertising helped create demand

Some thought that Jim should just dump pineapple on the market. Instead, he pondered over the situation briefly, then immediately headed for San Francisco and huddled with Hunt, Baumgartner, Jake Blumlein, Sussman, and the company's mainland sales force.

While there, he suddenly had an idea. Why not form a "cooperative association of advertising" with the other Hawaii pineapple canners and advertise Hawaiian canned pineapple as a "generic" product? This could be a joint marketing program by the Hawaii pineapple canners and would involve both industry-wide price cuts and a joint national advertising effort to "make the word 'Hawaiian' mean to pineapple what Havana meant to tobacco." Hunt and Sussman both liked it.

They decided to go ahead with the idea of the cooperative advertising, as it would take more money than Hapco could afford by itself, with an uncertain payoff. If it were to be put into operation, the risk would have to be shared by all. The rest of the competitive Hawaiian pineapple industry would have to cooperate.

Cooperation between competing companies was not a completely new idea in Hawaii. The Hawaii sugar companies had formed the Hawaiian Sugar Planters Association and had cooperated in the joint importation of labor, mainly from Asia. Labor had not been as much of a problem for the pineapple growers and canners, as there was already an ample supply of labor in Hawaii by the time the pineapple industry began.

In 1904, E. I. Bentley, who was then with the California Fruit Packers Association and later was to become president of California Packing Corporation, pointed out the advantages of industry teamwork at a meeting of the Agricultural Society of Hilo. He gave as an example the lowering of costs that could be gained by teamwork in importing pineapple plantation and cannery equipment.

John Emmeluth, Kidwell's partner in the formation of Hawaii's first cannery,

Eat Pineapple Pie

YOU'LL like it made from rich, juicy, Crushed or Grated Hawaiian Canned Pineapple. You don't know how good pie can be until you have tasted the incomparable flavor of the fully ripened fruit between layers of rich, brown, flaky pie crust.

Hawaiian Canned Pineapple
Crushed or Grated

is fully ripened in the semi-tropical sunshine of Hawaii and packed the same day it is picked, in sanitary, air-tight cans. The real pineapple flavor is retained. You will find it delicious for ice cream, ices, sherbets, sundaes, shortcake, salads and in dozens of other attractive ways.

Here is a good recipe for Pineapple Pie:

YOUR GROCER Sells CRUSHED or GRATED Hawaiian Canned Pineapple

Pineapple pie on Waikiki Beach

had also written of some of the advantages of cooperative efforts in the canning, warehousing and shipping of canned pineapples in the "Hawaiian Forester and Agriculturalist" in 1905. He thought that industry organization could prevent overproduction by controlling output and the numbers of individual canneries. At that time Jim, as leader of the industry, didn't see a need to band together with his competitors, but now he did.

Jim returned to the Islands and presented his concept to the competitors, seeking their financial assistance. All the packers were desperately trying to sell their pineapple and competition between them was keen. The idea that cooperation be substituted for the competition was not easily accepted. Some didn't like the fact that, since Hapco was larger than any of the other Hawaii canners, it would benefit the most. Also its name, the Hawaiian Pineapple Company, was closer to the name of the product they were promoting. Alfred Eames, of the

Jim was the first to offer recipes in advertising

CHAPTER THIRTEEN

Hawaiian Islands Packing Company was one who objected the most. He had been growing pineapple in Wahiawa long before Jim had purchased his 61 acre plantation, and he had also been a stockholder of Hapco before leaving to start a competitive enterprise. He may have felt antagonistic to anything Jim might suggest.

Jim laid out a map of the U.S. before the competitors showing all the cities where pineapple was yet to be sold, and somehow managed to persuade all but two of the pineapple packers to adopt his plan and to form "The Association of Hawaiian Pineapple Growers." The companies in the ad program were Hapco, Thomas Pineapple Company, Hilo Canning Company, Haiku Fruit & Packing Company (51 percent owned by Hapco), and Pearl City Fruit Company. The two companies who did not go along were the Hawaiian Islands Packing Company (Alfred Eames' company), and the Captain Cook Coffee Company, which packed pineapples as well as coffee.

or sliced, crushed and tidbits

Available sliced, crushed...

According to the plan, each company would contribute money to the program based on its individual case pack. Hapco, the largest, would contribute the most. A total of $50,000 was raised, and an advertising agency was hired by the Association to implement a plan. The amount raised was not much for a major national advertising effort, even in those days, but business was bad on the mainland and magazines were starving for ad space. "To say we were not concerned about the situation would not be the truth, but I will say we didn't lose our courage," Dole later said.

The Association of Hawaiian Pineapple Growers opened an office in New York City and salesmen called "drummers" were instructed to sell pineapple, and not to be concerned whose pineapple they were selling. Advertisements were first placed in trade magazines to be read by mainland food distributors, alerting the retail grocery trade and their distributors about the forthcoming promotion of pineapple and encourage them to participate in the promotional effort.

The notices advised the food distribution industry that the campaign was intended to promote the facts that not only were Hawaii's packing procedures the most sanitary in the world, but Hawaiian pineapple was superior to any other pineapple produced in the world. It portrayed Hawaiian pineapple as fully-ripened pineapple grown in the semi-tropics of Hawaii.

There was virtually no market for pineapple on the East Coast, although much of it was canned in Baltimore and Florida. On the West Coast, competition consisted of annual sales of 10,000 cases of Bahamas and Singapore pineapple and also pineapples from South Africa, Formosa (Taiwan), and Australia. Still, pineapples had done so well that many of the West Coast Grocers were currently selling more Hawaiian pineapple than the popular peaches. This evidence of the market strength of Hawaiian pineapple indicated that Hawaiian pineapple was indeed a superior product and that there would be both good sales and favorable gross profit margins for the grocers. The propaganda said that, "Hawaiian Pineapple is no more like other canned pineapple than a Baldwin apple is like a raw turnip," and, "Don't ask for pineapple alone, insist on HAWAIIAN pineapple."

After the publicity cam-

paign directed to the grocery industry, consumer magazine advertising was next placed in eight mainland periodicals on both on the West and East Coasts. The first ad was in Ladies World.

Pineapple at the time was not well known to the American public. Jim's grandmother thought they were "hard-apples." A market had to be formed from scratch. To sell more pineapples, the public had to actually be taught how to eat them, so pineapple recipes were given to show how they could be used. One ad said, "It Cuts With a Spoon - Like a Peach," and another, "It's So Dif-

Ads appeared in most popular ladies' magazines

Ads noted, "vigilant supervisors with blue ribbons around their caps are at every table"

ferent!! Picked Ripe!! Canned Right!!" The ads promoted both the product and the place where they were grown. They showed illustrations featuring Hawaii and displaying the growing and canning of pineapples in Hawaii. The ads also made the claim that other pineapples, such as the Red Spanish variety imported to Baltimore from the Bahamas, and the Singapore pineapple entering the U.S. markets, were inferior and just didn't have the quality of Hawaiian pineapple.

This advertising campaign represented Hapco's first major thrust into the Eastern markets. Although Hunt had all distribution rights, his marketing network was limited to the U.S. West Coast.

The advertising effort went beyond mere magazine advertising. For a six month period, the Alaska-Yukon Exposition of 1909 featured Hawaiian girls feeding sliced pineapple to thousands of visitors.

The advertising program was successful. Pineapple became a household delicacy, and the industry was formally established. Some years later, Jim said that had the industry failed to cooperate, and instead had panicked and unloaded their pineapples on the market, prices would have plunged 75 percent or more, and it would have been the end of the industry.

As for Hapco, though its profits increased through 1909, its earnings per share dipped for the first time in the company's history, and in 1910, the earnings per share were down 30 per cent. But by early June, 1909, the entire pack of Hapco's pineapple had been sold, and by 1911, profits nearly doubled.

Jim did not think that it was advertising alone that saved the company. He attributed Hapco's recovery from the depression also to the effective marketing efforts of its sales agent, Hunt Bros. Other contributing factors to the recovery were the decline in costs which came from having Hapco's new cannery adjacent to American Can Company's new can-making plant in Honolulu, and to Oahu Railway's pineapple delivery system from Wahiawa.

Still, the cooperative advertising ar-

This two color ad ran in 1929

Maile Gibson tasting pineapple in Jim's Wahiawa home.

rangement was significant. It was an accomplishment to unite an industry to market a single product, a big difference from a company marketing its own brand name. By its cooperation, the industry jointly initiated a selling policy which, despite large supplies of unsold pineapple, was maintained with discipline. Jim labeled it as, "The first associational campaign for a commodity."

Not only had Jim brought about the advertising campaign by being able to coordinate with his company's competitors a mass appeal to the ultimate users of the product, but he is attributed to being the first to advertise generic names in the food business. He is also attributed to being the first one to have the idea of advertising and offering recipes in women's magazines. This, Charles J. Bauman, later a senior vice president of Dole Food Company, thought was a major contribution.

The example of the pineapple industry in cooperative advertising was followed a few months later by the California orange industry.

Once the depression following the Panic of 1907 was over, and once the pineapple packs were successfully sold, the industry returned to stiff competition. The Hawaiian Pineapple Growers Association soon broke up because some of the members failed to pay their dues, but every time there was a crisis, they joined together again.

They did so in late 1912, when there was another financial crisis, which resulted in price cuts of about 20 percent by 1914. This time they called their association the "Hawaiian Pineapple Packers' Association," soon changing the name to the "Association of Hawaiian Pineapple Canners."

Another advertising campaign was launched in 1913, and continued through 1915, spending over $100,000 in total. This time Hawaiian pineapple again was advertised without concern about brand—"always ask for Hawaiian pineapple, no matter what brand, so long as it comes from Hawaii." The advertisements displayed diagrams instructing customers about the ease of opening a can of pineapple with a can opener, and how to serve the product.

Featuring the largest fruit cannery in the world

Brochures, as in the 1908 campaign, advertised Hawaii and its pineapple fields, and described how pineapples were grown and processed.

On November 16, 1916, there was a national celebration of "Hawaiian Pineapple Day" when restaurants, utilizing the recipes in the advertisements, featured pineapple on their menus. A song was composed in Honolulu to spotlight the day. It was called "Pineapple Rag," with words by James A. Dunbar and music by Alfredo Perez. The lyrics were:

"Talk about your Boston beans or hoe-cake
*   from the South,*
Or chicken a la Maryland that melts in
*   your mouth,*
There's nothing in creation or that's in the
*   eating line*
That can compare in flavor to the 'apple of
*   the pine.'*
CHORUS:
This pineapple, this pineapple, it's got me
*   going right,*
I call for it at breakfast and cry for it
*   at night,*
And every minute in between if you would
*   win my smiles*

Give me a juicy pineapple from the fair
*   Hawaiian Isles."*

The association went beyond advertising this time and engaged in cooperative experimental work in agricultural science. Jim looked at the funds expended for the cooperative efforts as a form of insurance in a rapidly changing technological industry.

Once the excess was distributed, advertisements again stopped, although cooperative scientific research efforts continued. Only when there was a problem with sales were cooperative ad campaigns reinstated. The longest ad program conducted by the industry was between 1922 and 1928. More recipes were introduced, including pineapple salads, pineapple desserts, pineapple breakfasts, cooked dishes with pineapple, and others. Industry advertising efforts faded again, but were renewed early in the depression, starting in 1931 with a $1.5 million budget. The health appeal of pineapple was emphasized this time, saying that the pineapple is comparable to the orange and the tomato in terms of vitamins A, B, and C.and that it helped prevent acidosis, etc.

Improvements on the Plantations

Suckers, slips or crowns are used as propogating material, and are planted through the paper mulch

Growing pineapples was not without its problems. There were problems in relation to soil chemistry, plant selection, plant disease, and agricultural techniques and methods. Jim always tried to find experts to find solutions to them.

One pest from the very beginning was the nematode. Hapco hired scientists who after many efforts, tried a fumigant called "DD" which helped, although nematodes continued to be such a problem that it was necessary to dig up the fields after a couple of ratoon crops and let them go fallow before replanting.

Jim persuaded the pineapple planters to cooperate in financing a research staff, which worked hand in hand with the Hawaiian Sugar Planters Association at the Territorial Experiment Station located in Wahiawa. The experimental station had a group of trained pineapple-oriented scientists that was cooperatively funded by the individual growers and packers of Hawaiian pineapple. At the

Experiment Station, the research scientists were organized into departments of pathology, genetics, nematology, chemistry, entomology and agriculture, and they continually sought better varieties of pineapple for canning, methods for controlling insects and plant diseases, and planting and fertilizing methods intended to increase yields and reduce costs. The group later developed into the Pineapple Research Institute. In 1925, the Association of Pineapple Canners purchased and moved the Institute to five acres of land next to the University of Hawaii with the approval of Dr. A. L. Dean, president of the University of Hawaii.

Iron deficiency was an unexpected problem in the iron-rich volcanic Hawaiian soil. Hapco discovered that although there was iron in the soil, as evidenced by the red dirt, the lower, darker and richer volcanic soils contained excess manganese which prevented the iron from reaching the leaves so that the

CHAPTER FOURTEEN

The asphalt paper-mulch being laid by machine

leaves turned yellow and the pineapples were deformed, small and sour. It was quickly found that the sick plants all suffered from iron deficiency.

The problem was solved in 1916 by Maxwell Johnson, one of the researchers at the Territorial Experiment Station in Wahiawa. He discovered a copper-like spray made by dissolving iron in sulfuric acid which furnished iron to the plants when sprayed on their leaves. The leaves absorbed the iron so that after the spray was applied, the yellow plants turned green. The spray was called "green giant." In order to reach thousands of acres of sick pineapple plants, the spray was applied to the pineapple leaves with long arm power spray capable of doing eight rows of pineapple at a time. The iron sulfate spray made it feasible to grow pineapple on marginal land.

In 1915, the plantation manager, John Whitmore, discovered that mulch paper, something like asphalt roofing paper, first used by the sugar planters, could be applied to pineapple cultivation for weed control, for conserving moisture in the soil, and for increasing the soil temperature which stimulated nitrate formation. The paper was called Eckhart paper, named after its inventor. The paper mulch was laid on the ground

to be planted and holes were punctured in the paper for the baby slips or crowns to be thrust in the ground through them. Use of the mulch paper greatly increased the yields of pineapple per acre. The Eckart paper mulch process was so successful that in 1922 Hapco, who had a patent on it, licensed its use to other Hawaii pineapple growers in return for royalty payments.

The development of Eckhart Mulch Paper, in addition to the iron sulphate spray, made it economically possible to develop the island of Lanai into a pineapple plantation, as the island would have been too dry without it.

Jim was always on the outlook, too, for improvements in harvesting techniques and machinery to handle the farming and processing of the rapidly increasing acres planted and tonnage harvested and processed. He felt that pineapple culture was closer akin to large scale horticulture than the more traditional agriculture, and its culture was specialized. This form of horticulture was new, and specialized equipment had to be invented. It was he who introduced trucks and tractors to the Hawaiian pineapple industry.

The current Hawaii crop is still a variety of the same Smooth Cayenne that the company grew in the beginnning. Jim encouraged the experiment station to try to develop new varieties, and during the 1920's attempts were made to develop pineapples which had the qualities wanted by "a selective field run." People went through the fields and marked the pineapples that showed the qualities they were looking for, and planting material from the marked ones were used for planting. Through this method some clones were developed by a "natural selection" process, so the industry has three or four varieties, all of which were the outgrowth of Jim's efforts.

Lanai pineapple, the F200, is a clone

Nitrogen, iron and zinc are supplied by foliar sprays

that is suitable for canning. The F200 is characterized by a uniform translucency, so that it ripens uniformly. It is also a "square shouldered" fruit rather than a tapered one, so that more slices can be canned. The Wahiawa pineapple, called "Champaca," is a clone selected for its suitability for the fresh pineapple market. Picked ripe, it has a longer shelf life than the F200.

The Pineapple Research Institute ceased to exist in 1972, and no new work is currently being done because the fields are too big, and even if a new variety were found, it would cost too much to convert an entire plantation to a new variety.

Both the plantation and the cannery have been served in terms of efficiency. Automation is one way to reduce the costs of labor, and ways to substitute labor by automation were made through the years in the plantations as well as in the cannery. Bulk fruit bins that would hold six or seven tons of fruit were substituted for lug boxes. Use of fumigants started in the mid-1930s. A mechanical harvester began to be used after World War II to replace hand picking and human muscle to carry the fruit. Now machines were used for harvesting, as well as forming the beds, applying the fumigants and laying the paper mulch in passes of three beds at a time.

Drip irrigation was developed, particularly on Lanai. Drip irrigation conserved water and improved yield consistency, and gave the company more control over the growing cycle so that all the pineapple didn't ripen at once.

Every field on Lanai is drip irrigated today. Production still peaks in the summer, but the peak is not as sharp as it used to be. A flatter peak allows the company to use its equipment better. Dole did as much as 70,000 tons a month in the peak season. "Now, we flatten that out," said plantation manager Jim Parker, to a steady 20,000 tons per month over the course of the year.

With pineapples ripening more evenly over the course of the year today than they used to in Jim Dole's time, the same output of pineapple can be produced with a smaller cannery.

CHAPTER FOURTEEN

IMPROVEMENTS IN THE CANNERY

Cannery workers waiting for the train bringing pineapple from the fields

The first machines used in canning were power driven but handled only three to five pineapples a minute after the peel had been taken off by hand. The original machine used was the Lewis Peeling Machine which was hand operated and, as a result, often took its toll of fingers and hands. It was essentially a revolving planer knife upon which the pineapple was centered by hand. Next used was the Zastrow Machine, which worked like a meat cutter. It was an improvement but was also slow.

Hapco employees made most of the inventions which improved Hapco's canning methods. One of Hapco's early patents was the Arnold and Hapco Slicing Machines developed by L.E. Arnold, a Hapco employee, and patented in 1909, which slices the whole pineapple into ring shaped pieces. Competitors paid Hapco royalty fees to use this greatly improved slicing technique.

Another employee invention was the Hill Slicer Feeder, developed by J. Hill

in 1915, a device for feeding pineapple into the Arnold Slicing Machine. Many of the machines, particularly in the cannery, were not unique to the pineapple industry, but their arrangement and coordination was.

In 1911, when a lot of pineapples were growing in the fields about ready to pick and the need for a machine that would process fruit more quickly was apparent, Hapco hired Henry Gabriel Ginaca to try to develop a machine that would peel, core, size, and trim pineapples. Ginaca was a mechanical draftsman who had been working for the Honolulu Iron Works Company. He also had been one of the original directors of Byron Clark's Tropic Fruit Company, so he had some knowledge about pineapple processing before joining Hapco.

Ginaca started with machines already being used, such as the Arnold Slicing Machine and the C.W. Cookson centering and holding device. His first two at-

The world famous water tank was designed in 1927

ning industry possible. Without such a machine it would have been difficult, if not impossible, to process all the pineapple that was coming in from the fields. Over the years the machine was improved until it could peel and core over 100 pineapples per minute. Hapco built Ginaca machines for its own use, but it also sold them to its competitors and never asked for royalties. Since Ginaca was an employee, the individual patents on his machine were assigned to the corporation. Until his resignation from Hapco in June 1915, Henry G. Ginaca was issued 11 U.S. patents on his pineapple machines, for a period of 17 years each.

Another employee invention was an "eradicator," which is an attachment to the Ginaca machine that scrapes the good fruit from the shell. Another was the Fisher Shell Machine, introduced in 1920 by G. E. Fisher.

In 1915, Hapco hired a chemist, the first professional chemist ever hired by the pineapple industry, Jim claimed later. The chemist's first objective was to improve the quality of the syrup used in canned pineapple. He also was to try to

tempts were failures. The first one was an upright machine that pushed pineapple out downward. Jim got so disgusted with it that he said that he would rather go back to the old method. However, in 1913 Ginaca met with success and invented a machine that handled about 35 pineapples per minute and eliminated the need to peel, core and pack them by hand.

The Ginaca Automatic Pineapple Machine was essentially a sizing and coring machine which made possible an automated process similar to Henry Ford's with his early automobiles. Pineapples reach the machine by a conveyor belt. The Ginaca chops off the top and bottom, cuts a cylinder in the pineapple leaving the peel, takes out the core, then slices what is left and delivers it to the trimming tables. Once through the Ginaca machine, the pineapple goes by conveyor belt to the trimming lines where it is cut to perfection before being canned. Before it goes to canning, it goes to a quality control area for final inspection, one of the six inspections the pineapple goes through during harvesting and canning.

The Ginaca machine was the breakthrough which made the pineapple can-

Final touches were applied at trimming tables

CHAPTER FIFTEEN

Ginaca machines to core and peel, were invented at Hapco

find ways to use pineapple by-products. Both objectives were achieved.

In the Ginaca machine automated process, the bulk of the pineapple was thrown away. What was left of the pineapple was about two-fifths of the original weight. Once the pineapple was safely canned, the remaining pulp, consisting of 50 percent of the pineapple, the shell, the core, and the trimmings, were at first piled up next to the cannery to collect flies and rot, and was later generally burned, dumped into the ocean or put into the fields as fertilizer. All of these disposal methods were expensive. In 1921, researchers found that the pulp could be put through shredders and cut into small pieces, and then pressed, dried, and put into the form of a bran. When supplemented with protein, the bran made a good food for livestock. By 1927, approximately 7,000 to 8,000 tons of pineapple bran were sold at a profit for feed for cattle, horses or pigs.

Of all the 39 pineapple canneries that started in Hawaii over the years, Hapco prospered because it was the most efficient, and thereby was one of the lowest cost producers. The new cannery, from the very beginning, had a constant stream of improvements in processing machinery. Hapco was responsible for introducing the bulk of all the specialized pineapple canning machinery utilized by the Hawaiian pineapple industry up to the time Jim Dole stepped down as president and chief executive officer of the company.

As more pineapples were grown, more had to be processed in the cannery. An additional 4.8 acres at the cannery site were acquired in 1920, increasing the total acreage at the cannery site to 18.8 acres. The company expanded the cannery site again in 1923 by buying more land in the vicinity. By 1931, the cannery had expanded to 30 acres. Then, instead of adding on to the cannery, the number of hours the cannery was operated was increased. During the peak harvesting season in 1925, the cannery for the first time used workers for six weeks in both day and night shifts. In 1926, the company operated day and night shifts throughout the peak harvesting season.

The daily capacity of the cannery to process pineapple grew to 26,125 cases, or 532,679 cans of pineapple. The record for a single day was 76,693 cases in 1926, a fruit canning world record. Hapco's cannery at that time was believed to be the largest in the world.

In 1929, a decision to increase the cannery's capacity was made, and $1.5 million was spent to expand and rebuild the plant to one with 48 processing lines and a capacity of 250,000 tons of fresh fruit per year, as compared to 112,000 tons processed in 1929. The new cannery had a total of 1.6 million square feet of floor space, or nearly 37 acres. Also on the drawing board for 1930 was a $250,000 pineapple juice plant.

On July 7, 1930, Hapco set another daily record at the cannery with the production of 94,085 cases. During the year a record 16,113 visitors toured the pineapple cannery.

When Hapco was building its bigger cannery and found that it needed a water tank for the automatic sprinkler system being installed, it decided to make it in the shape of a pineapple. Jim's wife's brother, Charles William Dickey, the

A production line of Ginaca machines. These machines made automatic processing possible

famous Honolulu architect and designer of the Alexander & Baldwin building, The Kamehameha Schools, and other Hawaii buildings, had first suggested the idea. Hapco's chief engineer, Simes T. Hoyt, provided the engineering drawings in August 1927, based on blowups of photographs of actual pineapples, and it was produced by the Chicago Bridge & Iron Works in Greenville, Pennsylvania at a cost of $16,500.

Tanks such as the Dole water tank had been used to advertise products before the Honolulu one was erected. Milk bottles, a light bulb, a loaf of bread, and a flower sack, Libby's beef stew, are among examples. Billboards were unpopular in Hawaii, even at that time, but there was no problem with a functional product feature. Hoyt also tried to get Hawaii to make its automobile license plates in the form of a pineapple, but the idea was never accepted.

The tank, which stood 80 feet above the cannery building, held 100,000 gallons of water and supplied the automatic sprinkler system by gravity. It weighed 30 tons and was 50 feet long, with a 22 foot crown. It was fabricated in three separate sections and supported by a steel tower coated with aluminum.

The purpose of the tank was not only to supply water to the cannery, but to advertise Hawaii as the "home of the pineapple." It tied in with the company slogan, "By Nature Crowned the King of Fruits." It was one of the first things a tourist visiting Hawaii saw when he arrived in Honolulu and one of the last things he saw when he left. It was clearly visible from Waikiki Beach and became a Honolulu landmark.

Originally the water tank was also intended to serve as a beacon for ships sailing in and out of Honolulu, for it was lighted by floodlights at night, but after other high rises were developed around the water tower, it could no longer be readily seen from the ocean.

CHAPTER FIFTEEN

UPS AND DOWNS, BUT MOSTLY UPS

Kaumalapau Harbor on Lanai. Jim bought the entire island for $1.1 million

In 1909 Hapco decided to spread out to the island of Maui by acquiring a 51 percent interest in the Haiku Fruit Company, which canned pineapples. To do this, the stockholders approved the issuance of another $100,000 of stock. Hapco and Haiku Fruit Company together would have a 60 percent share of Hawaii's pineapple output. This acquisition was completed on June 1, 1909 at a total price of $53,529, including cash and 981 shares of Hapco stock. It is possible that Jim's father-in-law, Charles Henry Dickey, who lived on Maui, influenced Jim to buy Haiku Fruit Company stock because C.H. Dickey's wife's brother, Henry Martyn Alexander, was a pineapple grower in the Haiku district of Maui. The company later sold this interest.

In 1914, there was again stiff competition and price cutting, and the price of a 2-1/2 tall can dropped from $.35 a can on the retail shelf to between $.10 and $.20. This time, the lower prices were offset by lower costs because the company was now growing most of its own fruit and buying very little from independent growers. This time, too, the low prices resulted in expanding the market for pineapple into Europe. While there was little buying from Germany, there was lots of buying from Britain.

Foreign buying from both Britain and France continued strong in 1915. Although shipping costs were higher during World War I, there was a 33 percent surge of sales.

Otherwise, prices continued weak and below production costs in both 1914 and 1915. Jim labelled these years as "a depression" in the pineapple industry. In 1916, however, pineapple prices started to go up 25 to 30 percent, and profits surged.

In 1917, after the U.S. entered into World War I, a major source of demand was from the U.S. military. Approximately 17 percent of Hapco's entire 1918 pack was picked up by the U.S. and Allied military sources.

After the war, demand for canned

Aerial view of Maui pineapple fields

pineapples continued strong, both in the United States and Britain.

At first Hapco bought much of its pineapples from other growers, but in time the company decided it would be best if it grew most of its own pineapples. Then it could control all operations of production from the plantation to the cannery level and thus insure quality. The pineapples could be "picked ripe and canned right." It would also allow the company to expand demand and deliver the product to the market at a minimum cost. Then the company was always on the outlook for more land.

In 1916, Hapco leased 3,767 acres of land from Waialua Agricultural Company. Then it acquired Hawaiian Fibre Company, which had a 29-year lease on 1,600 acres adjacent to Hapco's Wahiawa plantation. This acquisition boosted Hapco's pineapple land to 8,600 acres.

In 1916, the company started experiencing higher production costs in both cans and labor. Jim met the challenge partly by innovations that increased yields of pineapple per acre, so that the company didn't need to buy as much fruit from independent growers the next year.

By 1918, 85 percent of Hapco's pack was grown on its own plantation, up from 55 percent in 1916, and the company was processing a total of 33,500 tons of pineapple. The next year Hapco processed approximately 90 percent of its 44,500 tons of pineapple from pineapple grown on its own plantation.

In 1920, it bought another 788 acres of pineapple land in fee and leased 125 acres already planted in pineapple from the Lyman Estate in Wahiawa. By 1922, 93 percent of company's pack was grown on its own land.

With demand for processed pineapple exceeding supply, Hapco decided again to expand its plantation capacity in 1922. It boosted its land leased from Waialua Agricultural Company to 12,000 acres by purchasing a 17-1/2 year lease from

CHAPTER SIXTEEN

Waialua Agricultural Company, on which it had been paying $18 an acre a year, for $2.1 million which was paid for with Hapco stock. In need of cash in order to acquire the Island of Lanai, Hapco received from Waialua $1.2 million plus in cash in return for a total of 63,114 newly issued shares of Hapco stock at $52.80 per share. As a result, Waialua ended up with approximately one-third of the 189,060 Hapco shares outstanding. Jim and his board of directors thought the deal was good because it gave the company a total of 18,000 acres of pineapple land on Oahu at a time that more land was needed for pineapple as well as cash for future expansion needs. It turned out to be a mistake.

Jim then turned around and used $1.1 million of the cash he received from Waialua to buy the entire Island of Lanai. He figured that there were between 12,000 to 20,000 acres of prime pineapple land on Lanai — and it would all be under his control, a big leap from 40 acres at the time of incorporation in 1901.

Jim felt that with the company's combined land holdings, it could potentially triple its output of pineapple from its own plantations. Hapco processed 48,000 tons of pineapple in 1922. If its output tripled, it could process 144,000 tons of its own fruit. This compared with 70 tons in 1903.

The company was indeed growing. With the addition of Lanai, Hapco had expanded its pineapple acreage from 9,393 acres in 1921 to from 30,000 to 40,000 acres in 1922. Of about 89,000 acres of land in Hawaii suitable for pineapples, Hapco had nearly 45 per cent of the grade "A" pineapple lands in the Territory.

The 1923 year was particularly strong. There was a decline in the supply of canned pineapple and a high demand. Not only were prices higher than they had ever been, but Hapco had such good yields from the Oahu plantation, that it processed 40 per cent more pineapple than it had the year before. Jim Dole wrote in his 1923 "Report of the President and General Manager" to stockholders and directors "...that 1923 was an abnormal and perhaps phenomenal year in the pineapple business..." After 1923, there were ups and downs in pineapple prices, but they never reaching 1923 levels while Jim was Hapco's chief executive officer.

In 1924, prices declined again, 14 per cent, which led to a proportional decline in earnings per share for the company. To meet the declining margins, Hapco improved its delivery network to distributors so that less holding time was required for inventory.

Pineapple processed by Hapco increased 26 percent in 1925 to nearly 100,000 tons, which was equivalent to about 25 percent of the peach tonnage for the same year.

In 1927, prices dropped again, 11 per cent this time, because of a high inventory carryover from the previous year. Since prices had to be marked down to reduce supply, there was a 55 percent decline in 1927 earnings from the previous year. This time, the company responded to the weak prices by a national advertising program in women's magazines advertising Hapco's contribution to the Hawaii pineapple industry. This worked, so inventories were worked down and prices were increased about 11 percent the next year.

After a stable level of pineapple output from 1927 through 1929, output of tons processed increased over 40 per cent in 1930, when the company packed nearly 4.5 million cases of pineapple. Not only had yields of pineapple produced per acre increased because of improved scientific research, but the company now had a total of 25,143 acres of pineapple in cultivation.

LANAI

Lanai today is known as the "Pineapple Isle." Legend claims that the island was once the home of evil spirits and was uninhabited until a young Hawaiian prince drove the spirits away. The early Hawaiians used the island as a place of exile for "women offenders." Mormons and some ranchers settled on the island in the mid-1800s but didn't stay because of a lack of water. They left cattle, which along with the wild goats and sheep, slowly ate away the few remaining trees. Of the population that remained, consisting mostly of Hawaiian fishermen and their families numbering less than 100, all lived on the eastern side of the island. The leeward side was all cactus.

In the late 1800s Charles Gay and his family moved to Lanai and formed the Lanai Land and Development Company, acquiring all but 600 of the island's 89,000 acres from the Hawaii Territorial government and the Estate of W. M. Gibson (a Mormon settler) via a $250,000 stock offering in December 1896. The Gays hoped to develop a coffee plantation on the island. The Lanai Company cleared some of the land and drove most of the goats off the cliffs into the ocean. It first tried to grow sugar beets, the first grown in Hawaii, but gave them up because of a lack of water. The company started to drill a tunnel through the mountain from Maunalei Gulch, but didn't finish. Because it was losing money, the Gays then sold the Lanai Company to Frank and Harry Baldwin, ranchers from Maui, and principals at Alexander & Baldwin.

The Baldwins proceeded to develop a ranch and game preserve on the island. Gay remained on the island and formed the Gay Ranch to grow pineapples on the Baldwin land, with a contract to sell

The Kilauea brought over 140 officials and businessmen to the Lanai "Open house" in 1926

CHAPTER SEVENTEEN

The Territorial Governor, the Mayor of Honolulu and the Commanding General of the Hawaiian Department were present at the Lanai "Open house"

them to the Haiku Fruit & Packing Company. The Haiku Fruit and Packing company, a pineapple cannery on Maui, was controlled by Hapco from 1907 until 1918 when it was sold to Maui investors. The pineapple was first planted in 1911 in Nininiuai, located near Lanai City.

These pineapple plantings on Lanai sparked Jim Dole's interest in the potential of pineapple on the island. When he first visited Lanai in 1906 with a family friend, Albert Waterhouse, to explore its possibilities for growing pineapples, he found the island dry and dusty with severe erosion problems and wasn't interested. At the time there was still land available in the Wahiawa area of Oahu.

In 1918, Libby proposed doing a joint venture on Lanai with Hapco. Negotiations were in progress toward an agreement for Hapco to lease 5,000 acres if Libby bought and developed the island, but the matter was dropped.

Many of the pineapple companies were expanding to the outer islands. Both Libby and C.P.C. had expanded to Molokai indirectly by encouraging homesteaders to grow pineapple to sell to their canneries, the pineapples to be sent by barge to Honolulu.

Aware that more land was needed to meet rising demand for pineapple, Jim and John Whitmore checked out land owned by the Cooke family on the Is-

land of Molokai in 1919, which at the time became available for lease. Whitmore was for it but Dole was against it.

Then, in 1921, Dole and Whitmore went to Mexico, the Philippines, Fiji, San Domingo, Malaya, and Australia to check the pineapple growing possibilities. They came to the decision that Hawaii, in general, offered the best pineapple expansion opportunities in the world, and that although Lanai was a virgin land lacking an adequate infrastructure of roads, a harbor, labor, a water supply, and had a landscape covered with cactus, it was the best of the possibilities they had seen. It was only 60 miles away from the Honolulu cannery, and it satisfied all the basic requirements for climate, altitude, rainfall, and natural drainage.

They then set out with two land expansion objectives: to expand acreage in the Wahiawa area, where its existing plantation was, and to lengthen its leases from Waialua Agricultural Company; and to buy Lanai. Jim Dole later commented: "We bought Lanai to get room to grow in."

While the Baldwins had no intention of selling Lanai, they were interested in the Ulupalakua Ranch in upcountry Maui, which was owned by Dr. James H. Raymond. As a sugar company, Lanai was of little use to the Baldwins. Raymond wanted to sell the Maui property, but he was asking above the market price and would not sell for less.

Since Lanai was worth more as a pineapple plantation than as a ranch, Hapco was willing to pay a premium price for the Lanai property. Agent Harold Rice ran back and forth between the two parties, Dole and Baldwin, and finally put together a deal. Hapco was granted a three month option to buy the Lanai Company and the Gay Ranch for $1.1 million. Hapco decided to take the risk and bought the island in 1922. Through this purchase, Hapco acquired control of all but 600 acres.

Hapco made the purchase before it knew where the harbor was going to be. It then hired Francis Betts (Dry Dock) Smith, the most knowledgeable waterfront engineer in the country, to locate and design a harbor at Kaumalapau, Lanai. Dole relied on his old friend and former stockholder, Walter Dillingham, and his Hawaiian Dredging Company to handle the harbor improvements. The harbor was virtually blasted out of a cliff. The work involved the building of a 300-foot breakwater and a 400-foot wharf, and gave the harbor a minimum depth of 27 feet.

Before planting any pineapple, Hapco also spent about $1 million to pipe water from the rainy side of the island to where the pineapples would grow. It also built paved roads, and later, in 1926, it spent another $3.3 million on a water reservoir. By the end of 1927, what with housing and other improvements which had to be done, only 3,516 acres were planted.

When Hapco bought the Island for pineapples, most of the Hawaiian people living on the island didn't like the idea of working in the pineapple fields, so they moved to Lahaina, Maui. For workers, Hapco brought in men of Filipino, Chinese and Japanese extraction, mostly from Wahiawa and Hamakua, on the Island of Hawaii. The ethnic background of the Lanai islanders from that time on was mostly Korean, Japanese, Chinese, and Filipino. Pineapples then became the focus of life on Lanai.

After over $4 million of improvements had been expended on the Island, Hapco chartered an Inter-Island Steam Navigation Company steamship, the KILAUEA, on January 30, 1926, and held "open house" for 140 people, including the Territorial Governor, Wallace R. Farrington; the mayor of Honolulu, John H. Wilson; the Commanding General of the Hawaiian Department U.S.A., Major General E. M. Lewis; the president of the Honolulu Chamber of Commerce, George H. Angus; the president of the University of Hawaii, Dr. Arthur L. Dean; bankers, lawyers, engineers, physicians, public utility heads, plantation managers, various agricultural and horticultural experts, and other officials. Of course, along went Riley H. Allen and W.R. Chellgard of the Honolulu Star-Bulletin who covered the story fully in a 22- page hard covered book, titled "Lanai Island of Achievement." The guests were chauffeured around the Island in a caravan of Fords brought over for that specific purpose. Ample photos featured the harbor and the achievements there. A full account of the tour was covered in the book, including a gourmet buffet luncheon, "..that would have done credit to an exclusive New York club or to the long-vanished but never forgotten chef of old Delmonico's." The luncheon was followed by an address by Governor Farrington, endorsing the achievements of the Lanai project.

Hapco had converted the cactus covered island with 150 people and 4,000 head of cattle, into a productive hubbub of activity with up to 20,000 acres of pineapple-producing acreage along with about 1,000 pineapple workers and their families.

Hapco sold its pineapple under a number of brands, but did not use DOLE as a name. Jim avoided using the DOLE brand name, perhaps because his cousin Sanford discouraged him from publicizing a household name in Hawaii that had always been associated with religion and education.

Some of the brands included, Paradise Island, Hawaiian Club, Hapco's Best, Pacific Gems, Mauna Loa, Coral Reef, Outrigger, Fern, Treasure Island, Honey Dew, and Summer Land for its "Extra Quality" pineapple. "Standard Quality" brands included Panama Pacific, Plantation, Sea Island, Surf Rider, Ukulele, Waikiki, Palm Island, and Discovery. One of the early labels used in 1916 was "Hawaiian canned pineapple."

The company had done some advertising before the formation of the Association of Pineapple Growers. An August 20, 1906 letter from his cousin, Marian Dole Jones, who was living in Alameda, California said, "I received a post card from Agnes Judd (Albert Judd's wife) the other day with the label for your pineapple company printed on it. I am glad to see that it is going to be so well advertised. Such good pineapples as they are! I never ate such good ones as those you sent up."

In 1927 Hapco started to do some of its own advertising in addition to the advertising by the pineapple industry association. It used basically the same advertising approach as the industry had in 1908. It first announced in grocery trade journals that it was beginning a national advertising program, which was "supplementary to the advertising carried on by the Association of Hawaiian Pineapple Canners." All distributors of the product were again notified. The purpose was to make Hapco, as opposed to the Hawaiian pineapple industry, better known to the consuming public. The notification to the food industry boasted that "our company has from the first been the primary influence developing that industry."

The ads for the first time focused on the Dole name. While there was no Dole name as such until Jim Dole stepped down from the presidency of Hapco, advertising promotions at the time included language such as, "You can thank Jim Dole for canned pineapples." The ads went on to tell the consumer about the company's emphasis on the highest quality fruit.

Those developing advertising for Hapco suggested that "Dole" be used as a brand name because it was short and easily identified. The concept proved successful, and soon Hapco started us-

ing the "DOLE" name on all its canned pineapple. "DOLE" was stamped on the top of the can. In 1930, Hapco ads had DOLE written in large red letters across the text, and some of them said, "Look for DOLE stamped in the top of the can."

Jim also began to be in the limelight himself. While industry competition was stiff and Hapco's share of the canned pineapple produced in Hawaii declined from over 50 percent of the market in 1908 to between 30 to 35 percent in the late 1920s, the market was growing and by 1930, nearly 90 percent of all the canned pineapple produced in the world was from Hawaii. The Hawaiian pineapple industry contributed about $50 million to Hawaii's annual gross product and was the second largest industry in the Territory. Jim was the industry leader and it was his time of glory. He was the pineapple king. Every time he returned from a mainland trip, the press would announce his arrival with the grandeur of the most important of V.I.P.s. When his son, Dick, eloped to Las Vegas, the press featured the story with front page headlines for days.

CHAPTER EIGHTEEN

QUALITY AND ETHICS

Supervisor and worker inspecting sliced fruit

The statement, "We have built this company on quality, and quality, and quality" is in Jim's written "statement of principles" upon which he founded and operated Hapco. Incorporating these principles, the company developed into the first fully integrated agricultural company in Hawaii owning both vast acres of pineapple land and state-of-the-art processing equipment.

The company pursued all available scientific avenues in agricultural and processing technology. By 1921, Hapco owned 29 patents covering machines and processes in the pineapple industry, which represented virtually all of the specialized pineapple canning machinery. Most of these were developed by employees of Hapco. Dole made special efforts in employing and associating with those who were experts in their fields and would enhance the capabilities of the company. A key theory of Dole's was, "Don't try to do it yourself. Get an expert to do it." Considerable effort was

underway by 1925 to increase labor saving devices. Due to the care and quality the company pursued, canned pineapple was never questioned as being unsafe.

The image of quality that Jim Dole left in the industry has withstood the test of time. Industry sources today still speak about the quality of Hapco's product. Jack Larsen, pineapple industry consultant, claimed that while Dole was with Hapco, Hapco was the largest company in the industry and had the best quality.

There are only a handful of people who actually worked for Jim Dole still alive today. One of them is Lex Brodie. Lex met Jim Dole in the early 1940s, after Dole had stepped down from the position of president and general manager. Lex was then involved in quality control at the Honolulu cannery. While no longer with the company, Jim was still very much interested in what was going on with "his business," and would meet with Lex every time he visited from his home in San Francisco. With Lex,

Jim would begin at one end of the cannery in the food preparation area and go to the other, introducing himself to all he did not already know. There were two thousand employees there. Lex noted that one of the business principles he learned from Jim Dole that he applied to his own business endeavors after leaving Hapco was to always be on the job down where the action is and be "hands on management." "You can't run a business from an ivory tower. You need to talk to the people doing the work," he said. Lex also recalled that Jim Dole had a long term view of things, looking way down the road and because of this, led the industry.

Brodie later left the pineapple business and went on to form Lex Brodie's Tire Co. of Honolulu, of which he is president and sole stockholder. In addition to his tire company, Lex was the founder of Small Business Hawaii, a private non-profit organization in Hawaii advocating small businesses, in 1976. Services for members include small business forums and conferences, group medical benefits, consulting services, a small business resource center, etc. There were 3,000 members as of December 31, 1988. Today, some 45 years after first meeting Jim Dole, Lex retains a large picture of Jim in his office, and considers Dole as one of the "three wise men" in his life.

Jim also built his cannery on a solid base of the moral principles he had absorbed from his mother and father. "The Ethics of Progress" was the title of one of the books written by Jim's father, and published in 1909. Jim's background incorporated a philosophy that was an essential part of him throughout his business career. He was aware that the application of ethics in dealing with those around him was necessary in order to accomplish the development of a successful business enterprise. His objective was to humanize his business. His father said of him, "He sees the underlying relations which an honorable business bears to the great spiritual scheme of civilized society; he knows that business demands more than capital and is not measured by profits: that it is founded on the lines of thoroughgoing cooperation, and is interwoven with mutual respect and kindliness."

Father Robert Mackey, Professor of Business Ethics at Chaminade University in Honolulu, and one of the Chaminade founders, defines the ethical bottom line as "a partnership of workers and owners along with all other stakeholders in a humanizing corporate community of memory." What is important

Jim introduced himself to those he didn't already know

CHAPTER NINETEEN

> ## "We have built this Company on Quality – and Quality – and Quality."
>
> – JAMES D. DOLE, Founder, Hawaiian Pineapple Company, Ltd.

is how the corporation creates human value for all participants. Both ethics and economics are important in business. "The ethical bottom line is a humanizing partnership," according to Mackey. This is a partnership of workers and owners, along with all stakeholders. Stakeholders can include more than owners and employees. Stakeholders can include customers, community, suppliers, and competitors. "The community of memory is the living fruit of the past containing the life giving seed of the future," says Mackey. He claims that studies show that "the ethical investor in the long run does better."

Jim Dole recognized competitors as stakeholders for despite facing competition, he readily shared his secrets with others in order to further the growth of the industry. An example was his decision to sell Ginaca machines and other scientific breakthroughs of the company to competitors. Lex Brodie wonders to this day why the company ever sold the first Ginaca machine to its competitors. Another example was when Jim sold land to the City of Honolulu far below market price for the expansion of Queen Street.

Jim carried his emphasis on living ethics into his employee relations. His ideal was, "A square deal to every employee." He wrote: "I have been particularly interested in trying to organize our business in such a way that every employee, so far as possible, may feel that

his interest is that of the company and vice versa. I don't claim to have reached this point, but the recipe seems obvious; the Golden Rule, at least in the Confucian form, and preferably in the Christian version, backed up by the (biblical) quotation of Micah, 'What doth the Lord require of thee but to do justly, and to love mercy and to walk humbly before thy God.'"

Employee relations were important to Jim and he was very popular with his the workers. During the entire period he was its chief executive officer, Hapco never suffered from a labor strike.

"The payment of good wages and providing safe, healthful and morally wholesome conditions for the work in the factory and on the plantations" were prime objectives to Jim. Special pains were taken to assure that the cannery was well lighted and ventilated. An automatic sprinkler system was installed in 1921 to improve safety and protect the cannery from fire.

In 1915, the company for the first time set up a reserve for employees' compensation in accordance with the new federal Workman's Compensation Act. As a result of this Act, Hapco decided to carry its own Workman's compensation insurance. A pension plan was enacted in 1920, which contributed $25,000 to employee pensions. Hapco hired a trained nurse to visit the plantation villages. Efforts were made to spend money on labor saving equipment to reduce the amount of hard labor. Considerable money was spent in 1928 to improve the housing of plantation employees, so there came to be one-family cottages with lawns and gardens. By 1928, Hapco had a profit sharing plan as well as a pension plan.

Facilities put up in 1924 at the cannery included a dispensary, a locker and dressing rooms, and a restaurant. The dispensary was fully-equipped for first-aid with a trained nurse. Free medical service was provided each employee.

A cafeteria was provided where the employees could buy stew and rice for five cents, or a better meal for twenty-five cents. This was so that employees could enjoy full meals along with music to provide an "antidote for fatigue." There was also a shelter provided so that employees could eat their meals outside. There was a two-acre recreation field adjoining the cannery, completely equipped for baseball, basketball, volley-ball, etc. Since mostly women worked at the cannery, the company had a day-care center at the cannery for the children of the workers.

When the Island of Lanai was purchased in 1922, Hapco first built Lanai City to house the employees who would be working there. The intent was to build a "model village," complete with a store, a restaurant, a poolroom with a barber shop, a combination movie theatre and church, tennis courts, two baseball diamonds, a small hospital complete with a doctor and nurse, a bank, a clubhouse, and a power plant. Housing accommodations were made for about 750 people. The Koele Ranch on the Island provided a good supply of beef to the new residents. The excess was shipped to Honolulu for sale. Dole drew on his horticultural experience to have various varieties of trees planted on the Island, including trees from the company's own nursery.

Dole's treatment of workers is noted in various Japanese language newspapers. The Nippu Jiji claimed in 1921 that the company paid bonuses to each employee based on the number of years worked for the company. Bonuses were given in economic downturns as well as in times of prosperity. The article stated: "The Hawaiian Pineapple Company, Ltd. has set a new example in the relation between capital and labor, and the fact is worth noting." The Hawaii Hochi said in 1926 that, "Dole's methods of running the Hawaiian Pineapple Company is revolutionizing the sugar plantations' treatment of laborers. Because of Dole, the sugar plantations in Hawaii were compelled to improve their treatment of the laborers." Jim Dole told his youngest daughter, Barbara Larsen, that when he was getting started in the business, Edward D. Tenney, president of Castle & Cooke, "thought that he (Jim Dole) was a Communist."

Employee ownership of Hapco grew after the 1907 public stock offering. Out of a total of 448 stockholders in 1919, and 507 in 1920, a constant 11 percent was held by employee stockholders. A program was introduced in 1921 to facilitate further employee purchases of Hapco stock. This program was set up with employee stockholder loans amounting to $57,000 in 1921, whereby employees would borrow from the company to buy their company's stock. This may have been one of the first employee stock ownership plans in existence. In 1921, out of total shares, employees owned 31 percent. Out of 797 stockholders in 1922, 30 percent were employees. Employee ownership of Hapco stock peaked in 1924 with 38 percent of all of Hapco stock owned by employees.

Jim also promoted pineapple products to employee-owners. When there was a price decline and resulting margin squeeze in 1921, Jim tried to get employee-stockholders to be actively involved by eating more of the product.

Based on Jim's principles of quality and morality, Hapco managed to stay ahead of vigorous competition in terms of market share, profitability, growth and technology. According to an observation by Castle & Cooke, "Hawaiian Pine was the first successful pineapple canning enterprise in the world... (and) the leader of the development of the industry.."

CHAPTER NINETEEN

JIM AND HIS FAMILY

Charley, Jim, Betty, Dick, Barbara, Belle and Jimmy. Taken around 1917 or 1918

When Jim's business picked up, after his first years farming at Wahiawa, so did his social life. In order to get to town quicker, in spite of his shaky finances he bought one of the earliest cars in Hawaii. His license number was 6.

Jim's sister Winifred, or "Win," decided she didn't want to go to college and persuaded her father to send her on a trip to Hawaii instead. Full of high spirits and fun, she added new dimensions to Jim's life. She joined a rowing club that rowed in Honolulu Harbor and persuaded a friend whom she had met, Belle Dickey, to join. It was Win who introduced Jim to Belle.

Belle was a grandaughter of one of the missionaries to Hawaii, William Patterson Alexander, whose son Sam was the Alexander who started Alexander & Baldwin, Inc. She had grown up on Maui horseback riding with her Baldwin cousins, had been away to school in California and New York, had travelled in Europe, and was now one of the beautiful young ladies of Honolulu society. Jim fell in love with her.

As it happened, Belle was engaged at the time to someone else who was away studying at a divinity school and who later was a missionary in China. Jim faced this problem in his usual indomitable way. He wrote the other young man, telling him of his desire and intention to marry Belle, and the man freed Belle from her ties to him.

Win and Belle played tennis and hiked and went horseback riding together, sometimes at Wahiawa. Once Jim took them on a trip around the island, on which they had many flat tires which Jim had to repair on the spot. He often joked later that Belle had fallen in love with him because of his car.

Before long Belle and Jim were engaged. In 1906 Belle travelled to the mainland to visit cousins in California and then joined Jim on a trip to Boston to meet his parents. Belle didn't go with the intention of being married, but when they got there, urged on by Jim's parents, they decided that it was the sensible thing to do. They were married by Jim's father, Charles, in his Jamaica Plain church on November 22, 1906. Since Belle hadn't expected to be married on the trip, none of her family was with her, but on their return, Belle's mother had a big reception.

By this time Jim had ordered a prefab cedar house which he had added on to the original one-room shack at Wahiawa. The rooms were small and dark, but had atmosphere. He and Belle lived in it the first year of their marriage, then moved into Honolulu, along with the cannery, to live in the house they built on Wyllie Street in Nuuanu Valley, using the plans given them as a wedding present by Belle's brother Will, an architect. About this time, Jim sold over 900 of his shares of Hapco stock, perhaps to pay for his new family expenses.

The first baby, Richard Alexander Dole (Dick), was born on October 28, 1907, and named after Jim's brother. He was followed by James Drummond Dole Jr. (Jimmy) on February 6, 1910, Elizabeth (Betty) on April 25, 1911, Charles Herbert (Charley) on October 30, 1914, and Barbara on October 10, 1916, all born in the house on Wyllie Street.

Jim was baffled with his first children, who weren't always as well behaved as they might be, but by the time Barbara and Charley arrived, he was more used

Jim bought one of the first cars in Hawaii. His license number was 6

to children. Both seemed unusually smart and attractive, and they were the apples of his eye.

In about 1920, when the problem with the pineapple company was with sales rather than production, Jim found that he was needed more in California than in Hawaii, so he moved the family to California for two years. For a while, Belle and the children stayed with her mother and father in Piedmont. Across the street was a park, where Dick played at being Tarzan, running around barefoot trying to toughen up his feet.

Not only were Belle's parents living in Piedmont, but also her brother Will, the architect, and her sister, Grace. Eventually Jim and family moved into a house near Grace's on Highland Avenue, and the older children and Charley were put in school.

While the family was living in Piedmont, the flu epidemic hit the country. Belle and the children were scheduled to go for a vacation to Lake Louise in Canada. Belle didn't feel well when they started, but went anyway, and when they arrived, she had the flu and most of the others came down with it. Jimmy had such a high temperature that he became delirious. The whole family was quarantined in their hotel room until they recovered and then left for home in Piedmont. Belle vowed to never again start on a trip if she weren't feeling well.

Back home, poor health continued in the family. The children came down with swollen glands. Belle's and Charley's ears became infected and both had mastoid operations. Following the operation, Belle was deaf in one ear for the rest of her life.

Jim was not always easy to live with. For one thing, he often made decisions without consulting those concerned. Belle was upset after she took the children to California for what she thought was a visit, to find that Jim expected them to stay for two years. She was further upset when she found he had rented the Wyllie Street house in Honolulu without consulting her. Jim was always very polite and nice to his wife, but he didn't pay much attention to her ideas. Only when he was older was she able to influence him and then was surprised to find that she could.

Jim always thought his wife was too extravagant, but to a "thrifty yankee," whose father once turned down a raise in his own church, most people were extravagant. He never spared money for medical expenses, education, or anything he considered important, but the children grew up feeling that it was wrong to spend money. By the time the children were in high school, Jim had adequate means, but none of the children grew up thinking they were wealthy.

While they were in California, Jim sold the land surrounding the Wyllie St. house and Belle thought that without the land, she no longer wanted the house, so they sold it too. The company was now doing so well and Jim's salary had increased so much that he bought a beautiful big home on five acres of land on Green Street on the slopes of Punchbowl. When the family returned to Honolulu, they moved into the Green Street home and lived there until Jim left the pineapple company and they moved to the mainland.

One entered by a driveway which went from the entrance to a porte-cochere in front of the house. Another road from the entrance went to the back of the house and the garage. There was a greenhouse full of orchids, and an aviary full of canary birds. Behind the garage were pens for chickens and a shed for cows which furnished milk for the family.

The grounds were taken care of by a head gardener, Ah Kui, who lived in quarters over the garage. There were also two additional gardeners, who lived in shacks in back. There was a cook and his wife who had quarters near the kitchen. The cook's wife was the downstairs maid, and Ah Kyau, who slept in one of the bedrooms upstairs, acted as the upstairs maid. The family also had a chauffeur, Howard Ho.

The front door opened into a big front hall with parquet oak flooring. A beautiful staircase curved up to the second floor, at the bottom of which there was always an orchid plant covered with white blossoms. To the left was a little library, full of books. Off to the right was a parlor with a grand piano, other elegant furniture and one of the latest models of phonographs. There was also a dining room and pantry. Off the dining room and parlor was a porch with a pingpong table and wicker furniture. In front of the house was a big lawn with thick manienie grass down a slope, which the children loved to slide down on kiddie cars and later rode down on bicycles.

Upstairs were five bedrooms for Belle, Ah Kyau and the children. Jim slept away from the others in a big round room on the third floor, which had a wonderful view of the city and ocean. He could see the ships as they passed Diamond Head and, if he was to meet someone on one of them, he knew just how long it would take him to get to the dock to be there when it arrived.

Here the family lived while the chil-

Jim and Belle receive a family welcome

dren grew up. Howard would chauffeur them off to Punahou school and pick them up and take them to their various appointments. When Belle and Jim were away, there would be governesses to take charge. When Betty was in high school, her monthly dancing classes given by a Madame Lester took place in the house.

Each summer, the family moved out to the Wahiawa house to spend the summer, and once they were there, they rarely left until the summer was over, because it was still a long ride in the car over the dirt roads to Wahiawa, twenty-five miles away. Sometimes the roads were so muddy that chains had to be put on the tires. Even with chains some of the steep roads in the Waikakalaua and Kipapa gulches were dangerous when they were muddy. At Wahiawa, Ah Wo would do the cooking. There were old nags for the children to ride, books to read, trees to climb and the outdoors to investigate.

After a few years, Jim leased land and built a two story house on Kahala beach some five miles from town, next to houses of friends and relatives. On one side was a house owned by Maude and Platt Cooke, on the other the Frank Ather-

tons. Closer to Black Point was the John Waterhouse place. The family went there on Easter and Christmas vacations and sometimes for picnics during the year. The house was located on an unpaved road that is now Kahala Avenue. The whole area was covered with kiawe trees, which often blew down in kona storms. At that time it was considered enervating to live all the time at the beach.

Later still, Jim bought a lot on Kailua beach, where he put up a shed with restrooms and showers, and the family went there sometimes to picnic and swim.

When in town, the entire family went to church on Sundays at Central Union Church, the New England missionary Congregational church. Jim was not active in the church, but church was part of the family routine.

When Belle wasn't off on a trip with Jim, she was kept busy bringing up the children, managing the house, entertaining and being entertained. Many were the dinner parties, teas and dances at the house. She also had her own hobbies. She took bridge lessons and played bridge with her friends. At one time, she and Martha Waterhouse, her cousin and good friend, made hats and lampshades and painted and put glitter on them. She also became an expert knitter.

When Waialae Golf Club opened, Jim and Belle joined and Belle became an inveterate golfer. Jim had played golf while growing up in New England and occasionally played golf as an adult, but he never developed Belle's enthusiasm. He once told Hapco vice president, Deane Malott, that the golf pro recommended to him that, "he had nineteen major faults and twenty-three minor ones and as soon as these were corrected, he would be an excellent player." Perhaps because she played a good game of golf, Jim liked to say, "She is a powerful woman" and "I wouldn't like to have her hit me twice."

Belle made much of Christmas. She

was busy for months ahead buying presents. Each year she decorated a big tree in one corner of the living room at Kahala and put up sheets to hide it until the big day arrived. On Christmas day, after they had opened the gifts in their stockings, when the children went downstairs, there would be the beautiful tree stacked with presents. In the morning Santa Claus would arrive, jingling his bells all dressed up and carrying a big bag of presents, which he would pass out to those present. A big family dinner followed.

Sanford Ballard Dole often came to the family Sunday and Christmas dinners. One year he took the part of Santa Claus, which was appropriate because of his big white beard. Unfortunately his beard caught on fire, but most of it survived.

Although Jim and his brother Richard loved sailing while growing up on the east coast, Jim was too busy with the pineapple company to get involved in recreational activities in Hawaii. "He just didn't have time," according to Charley. However, when his wife's niece's husband, Earl Thacker, encouraged Jim to buy a sailboat so that Dick and Charley could learn to sail, he did, and both boys became enthusiastic sailors.

Jim was good to strangers. When the navy fleet came to town with cruisers and battleships, he would sometimes encounter a sailor and bring him home for dinner. Charley remembers a couple of sailors who became family friends.

Jim loved his family but was too busy and involved with his company to be around much. He not only worked long hours, and sometimes on weekends but was often away on trips. He would usually arrive home late but in time to have dinner with the family. Sometimes he spent time working in his room, but was always down for meals. After dinner he would retire to his special chair on the porch.

Belle with Jimmy, Charley, Betty & Dick in 1915

Charley and Barbara spent more time with him than any of the other children, especially when the others were away at school or college. They sometimes played mah jong with him, and he would read poetry to Barbara.

Occasionally Jim would take Charley with him when he drove around the Wahiawa pineapple fields. Charley remembers how he would talk to the workers, and knew most of them by name. In town, Jim often took Charley to football games on Saturdays, and on Christmas day, Jim took the boys to the football games, in which a visiting team from the mainland played the town team. He was a football fan and was proud of Dick and Charley when they played tackle on the Punahou football team.

Jim was conscientious in relation to the children, and when he was away, he always wrote letters to them, but he was inclined to think that children should be seen but not heard, and he didn't like to be interrupted. He was critical, but always ready to give compliments if pleased. His son Dick remembers him as being a boss at work and at home. What he said was it, and he didn't consult his family. Jim tried to reason with the children, which didn't work, and he had a way of moralizing which didn't go over well. Barbara remembers playing mah jong with him, and when he took risks and lost, he would point out the dangers of taking risks.

He was easily irritated. The family had two dogs, a fox terrier and an airdale. When they barked, he would shout at them, which upset Betty, as she was fond of the dogs.

Jim expected his sons to go into business. Charley said that his father expected him to "work like hell and be a businessman," and so he grew up expecting to be a businessman. Both Charley and Dick majored in economics at Stanford. "That was the way I was expected to go," said Charley. Later Charley got his MBA at Harvard Business School, which pleased his father because Harvard was his school and none of his other sons had gone there.

In college, Charley decided that he would never work for Hapco. Although he didn't think that his father would have been a hard taskmaster, he figured that he would have continually lectured him and would have expected him to work harder than anyone else. Charley considered himself a little lazy, and that kind of pressure didn't appeal to him.

Jim also expected a lot of Barbara and she said it was a "terrific burden" on her. "Father expected me to be wise beyond my years, trustworthy, and to use common sense." He encouraged her and gave her the impression that she was the smartest of the children. If she wrote a poem, he was very proud of it and would pass it around at work. Barbara felt she learned her value system from him.

"Father was an artist as a businessman and taught me respect for creativity," she said. He had a strong conscience, which he passed on to his children. She also learned to appreciate intellect from him.

Later, when Barbara was in college and afterwards, she became sympathetic towards the Communists and she was generally pro-union and politically radical. Jim was a Republican and against the "New Deal," and he would merely listen with his mind already made up, but he was tolerant and appreciated the fact that she was socially conscious and thinking for herself. She said he was a good listener.

No book about Jim would be complete without mentioning his ability to tell jokes. He not only enjoyed telling funny stories, but was probably one of the best at it in the islands. He had both an extensive repertoire and a wonderful sense of timing. He could keep all at a dinner table roaring with laughter. His children had favorite stories which they would beg him to tell again and again.

Jim went on many steamship trips to California and back. On these trips he would tell his jokes, learn the names of the young ladies, probably dance with them, try to sing the latest songs and generally be the life of the party. After returning to Honolulu, he would have a tea party for his friends from the ship who were always delighted to come.

Jim pretended that he had a special love for pigs, which he didn't have at all, and if he saw one, he would oh and ah and pretend to be overcome with admiration. As a result people were forever giving him pig figurines of one kind or another.

Every year for a while, he sent little boxes of chocolate candy to a list of friends, who appreciated them even though they often arrived melted.

Many, many people still remember Jim with fondness. When Betty was at a 1989 sixtieth reunion festivity of her husband's class at Punahou, the husband of one of his classmates turned to her and said, beaming, that he had worked at Hapco, and her father had "always joked" with him. When she tried to pin him down, he said that he had been in charge of collecting the signatures on the meal tickets, and Jim would pretend that he was putting his signature on an important document and ask him if he was sure it was all right to sign.

THE DOLE DERBY

Art Goebel, pilot of the winning plane, receiveing flowers before takeoff

The successful flight of Captain Charles A. Lindberg across the Atlantic Ocean from the United States to Paris on the "Spirit of St. Louis" thrilled people all around the world and made him a hero. Soon, the idea of airplanes flying from the United States to Hawaii entered people's minds. The 2,500 mile trip across the Pacific Ocean from the West Coast to Hawaii was the next challenge.

The Hawaii Governor, Wallace R. Farrington, and Star Bulletin Editor, Riley Allen, got the idea that a race from the West Coast to Hawaii would give the islands desirable publicity. They went to Jim to discuss the idea with the suggestion that he be the sponsor. Jim could see that the publicity from such a race could be good for pineapples as well as for Hawaii, and he also saw the advantages in air service between Hawaii and the mainland. So, on May 25, 1927, he made an offer of $25,000 for the first plane, and $10,000 for the second, to arrive in an air race from the mainland to Hawaii, if held within the next one year and three months. The offer was out of his own pocket and did not involve Hapco. The race, called "The Pacific Venture," was touted as the beginning of transpacific air service.

Jim had no personal knowledge about flying so he brought in experts to handle the affair. He turned it over to a "Contest Committee" to establish safety regulations and to qualify pilots. Jim was purposely not a member. He was only the financial sponsor. The only Hapco official involved was Harry E. MacConaughey, vice president and San Francisco manager. On the committee were Clarence H. Cooke, president of the Honolulu Chapter of the National Aeronautics Association (NAA) and president of the Bank of Hawaii, representatives of the Navy, the NAA, and the director of aeronautics of the Department of Commerce. Much of the responsibility for regulating the event was taken over by the NAA, an organization which predated the CAA and the FAA and was authorized by the U.S. Department of Commerce to govern all aerial sporting events.

Fifteen pilots immediately signed up for the race. Lindberg was not one of them, though some thought that he might enter as the route from Oakland, California to Wheeler Field on the island of Oahu was shorter than the 3,600 miles he had flown to Paris.

The flight date was set for August, 1927 to give the committee time to make their plans for the race. One of its decisions was that each pilot must hold a Federation Aeronatique International certificate and an annual NAA license.

Two airplanes did not wait but started off for Hawaii before the race was to start. Lester Maitland and Albert Hegenberger of the Army Air Service, flew from California to Wheeler Field in central Oahu in a Fokker tri-motor aircraft in 25 hours and 49 minutes on June 28. A couple of weeks later, Ernest Smith and Emory Bronte flew from Oakland, California to Hawaii in a Travelair single-engine monoplane, and crash landed on the Island of Molokai. These early flights took the glamour out of the Dole flight since now none of the planes participating in the Dole flight race would be the first to land in Hawaii, but their flights showed that such flights were possible, and perhaps made people less cautious.

Participants were from all over the United States, including one from Hawaii, Martin Jensen:

Martin Jensen (26), a 2,500 flight hour veteran, flying a Breeze monoplane, the "Aloha." The Aloha received financial backing by certain Honolulu businessmen.

Bennett Griffin (31), flying a Travelair monoplane, the "Oklahoma," financially backed by a group of Oklahoma businessmen.

Arthur Goebel (31), a movie stunt

Art Goebel and Martin Jensen receive their prize money at the Royal Hawaiian reception

flier, flying a Travelair monoplane, the "Wollaroc." His financial sponsor was Frank Phillips, the founder of Phillips Petroleum Company.

Major Livingston Irving (31), a World War I flying ace, then living in Berkeley, California. His plane was a Beeze monoplane, called the "Pabco Pacific Flyer," and was backed financially by the Paraffine Company of San Francisco.

Capt. William P. Erwin, a resident of Dallas, Texas, flying a Swallow monoplane, called the "Dallas Spirit."

John (Auggy) Pedlar (24), a resident of Flint, Mich., and a veteran of 4,000 flying hours. His plane, the "Miss Doran," a Buhl biplane, was named after Mildred Doran, a pretty school teacher with a love for flying. Mildred was the only actual passenger on the Dole flight. This entry was backed financially by William Malloska and the Lincoln Petroleum Co.

Lt. Norman A. Goddard (32), a resident of San Diego. His plane was a monoplane, the "El Encanto."

Jack Frost (29), a Wall Street bond salesman and flying enthusiast, experienced in wing-walking and other avia-

August 16, 1927. The start of The Dole Derby

tion stunts. He was financially sponsored by William Randolph Hearst's newspaper chain in flying a Lockheed Vega monoplane, the "Golden Eagle."

Seven other planes were unable to leave the starting block. Three of them crashed before ever arriving in Oakland for the start. A fourth was disqualified by the National Aeronautics Association because it didn't have enough fuel capacity to reach Hawaii.

Jim got very worried when three of the planes crashed before the race even began, and he requested tighter safety features. The National Aeronautics Bureau agreed. Thus, in spite of necessitating a further delay, new regulations were announced. The planes were required to have extra gasoline tanks, and each plane would have to be accompanied by a qualified navigator. A board of examiners was formed to test the navigational abilities of each navigator. Also, steamships in the area were asked to keep an eye on the passing planes. Only two of the planes had two-way radios, the Wollaroc and the Oklahoma. None had blind-flying instruments.

Now the flyers had to locate navigators. Jensen advertised in the San Francisco newspapers for one. The first applicant's qualifications included finding his way out of the woods after being lost. Jensen finally chose Paul Schluter, who was employed as a navigator on a commercial ship. This was Schluter's first flight, but he passed the NAA navigational exam. The equipment he brought along for the flight included a sea sextant, a spyglass, a flashlight, and a Bible.

The race on August 16th was started at noon to allow a daylight arrival time in Honolulu the next day, with an official and a starting flag at the 7,000 foot runway at Oakland, California, the present site of the Oakland International Airport. A crowd of approximately 200,000 people were there to watch.

The Oklahoma was the first to go, followed by the El Encanto. The El Encanto couldn't get off the ground. It ran off the runway and smashed its landing gear, which put it out of the race. Next followed the Pabco Pacific Flyer, which cracked up on the runway before taking off, but no one was injured in the incident. The Golden Eagle, the Miss Doran, the Aloha, the Woolaroc, and Dallas Spirit followed with successful takeoffs. The Dallas Spirit returned with a damaged fuselage, and resigned from the race. The Miss Doran flew back to replace spark plugs and was off again. The Oklahoma limped back with engine failure and dropped out of the race. This reduced the fleet to four as the audience stared into the fog waiting to see if any more came back.

Jensen said that he flew up to 4,000

feet, trying to get above the fog at a top speed of about 110 miles per hour, but couldn't do it. He couldn't tell whether he was up or down, and then got into a spin. He realized the plane was near the water when the undercarriage of the plane hit a wave. He recovered about 100 feet above the water and continued on just above the water until he was out of the fog. The next crisis was when they almost hit a steamer ship.

After flying all night, Schluter tried to get a celestial fix as to where they were navigating with his sextant at high noon. He finally realized that they had missed Hawaii and were flying beyond the Islands. He told Jensen of this problem, and that they might soon be running out of fuel, by passing a message along a clothes line strung on pulleys connected to the gas tanks. After fixing their position, they headed back to Hawaii through the Kolekole pass and landed safely at the Wheeler Field finish line. They had only enough fuel left for about 20 minutes of flight time. Schluter grabbed his Bible and sextant and hopped off the plane vowing never to fly again. He was going back to sea.

The race was won by the Woolaroc, the only remaining participant equipped with a radio. Following the radio beam, Goebel had no trouble locating the islands. The winning time was about 26 hours. The Aloha's second place time was a little over 28 hours.

The pilots, their spouses, and the crowd of 75,000 at Wheeler Field, including Jim Dole's family, who had arrived at 5:30 A.M., waited for the other two planes in the reviewing stand. They waited, and waited, and waited. Finally the Navy launched an air and sea search for the missing planes. Hearing the news, Erwin, who had been forced out of the race, took off with his Dallas Spirit to aid in the search, but he, too, was lost. None of the missing planes or their crews were ever found.

A luau was held at the home of Jim Dole on Green St. the evening of Aug. 19th. As a result of the lost fliers, the luau guest count was scaled back to about 30. The official presentation of the awards at the Royal Hawaiian Hotel on historic Waikiki Beach the morning of August 21st was much more sober than originally expected. There was little celebration. Attending the event were Governor Wallace Farrington, Walter Dillingham, Jim Dole, Clarence H. Cooke, the general manager of the Royal Hawaiian Hotel, among others. There were a total of about 150 present, mostly guests of the hotel.

There were a total of 10 lives lost as a result of the Dole Derby. The San Francisco Examiner, owned by Hearst Newspapers, offered a $10,000 reward to anyone finding survivors from the race. William Malloska offered $10,000 for anyone finding the Miss Doran or its survivors, and Jim Dole offered $20,000 for survivors from either of the lost planes.

During the next few days, the press began to get critical about Jim. The Sacramento Daily story quoting from California Lt. Governor Burnon R. Fitts, likened the event to stunt flying. Jim agreed that the race was a mistake, and later recollected that, "I had no idea that there were so many damned fools who were willing to risk their necks in old crates made of flour sacks and fishing poles."

Jim can't be blamed for the tragedy any more than the fliers themselves or the Hearst Newspapers, Phillips Petroleum, Lincoln Oil, the NAA or others. All recognized the risks involved, especially since the race was marred with tragedy even before it began.

The race established the value of radios in aviation. It gave a boost to the development of air flights to Hawaii, and it showed the necessity of flight safety regulations. Nevertheless, it did leave a sour taste in everyone's mouth and a mark on Jim's credibility and career.

CHAPTER TWENTY-ONE

THE PENNASK LAKE FISHING CLUB

Jim and Belle at Pennask Lake

At times during his life, the pressure of business would become too much for Jim and he would become very depressed. When this happened in the mid 1920s, his doctor advised him to get away to relax, and he particularly recommended fishing.

When Jim had gone on business trips in the early years of the pineapple company to investigate new equipment and canning processes used in the Alaskan salmon industry and the Pacific American Fisheries, his interest was aroused in big game hunting in the Pacific Northwest.

Jim admired the enterprise he witnessed in the Northwest on one of his visits to Alaska in 1916: "That is something with which one is immediately impressed in Alaska, the vitality and earnestness of the men, all of whom are doing something and going right after it. Neither do they take themselves too seriously."

Taking the doctor's advice, Jim and Belle first started out by fishing for salmon. Then they traveled to British Columbia to hunt Caribou in the Rockies, and to fish in the lakes there. On one vacation, the thought came to Jim to join with friends and family and have their very own lake where they could fish in peace from the outside world.

Jim contacted Canadian agents, a Mr. Irvine, Mr. Peck and Robert Simpson, to search out a secluded lake somewhere in the Northwestern wilderness. Then someone suggested he look up a Mr. and Mrs. Robert Cowan, partners with Alex Philip at a lodge at "Fish Lake." The Cowans recommended two lakes that would satisfy his requirements, "Big Bar Lake" and "Pennask Lake."

Jim and Belle liked best the description of Pennask Lake, which was located in southern British Columbia between Vancouver and the Selkirt Mountains, about 30 miles east of Merritt. They scheduled a field trip to tour the site in September, 1927. After driving as far as they could out of Merritt with Mrs. Cowan and two hired hands, they completed the remainder of the journey on horseback, accompanied by a wagon train. Eight and one–half hours later, struggling through a maze of granite boulders, the party finally arrived at the lake.

It was a beautiful spot, heavily wooded, and dominated by Pennask Mt. at an elevation of 6,000 or 7,000 feet. When they went fishing, Jim caught twenty-one trout and Belle caught fourteen. Upon returning to shore, they ran into an "old timer" who had fished in the area since 1900. He claimed that back in 1900 it was customary to catch as many as 500 trout over a two- to three-day period. Other than he and a few Indians, Pennask Lake was not fished. Jim decided he had arrived at the right spot.

There were a total of 2,100 acres of land along the lake front and the islands on the lake, and one individual cattle rancher owned the land adjacent to the lake. After some inquiry, Jim found that the Lake was available for purchase as either homestead land or "Crown Grant Purchase," in units of 640 acres at $2.50 per acre. The Cowans estimated that if there were a lodge at the site, operating costs would approximate $10,000 to $12,000 a year, and it would cost about $2,500 to upgrade the access road.

Upon returning to Vancouver, Jim retained a Canadian law firm to draw up land claims to include the 320 acres of ranch land that fronted the lake. The price on some of the land immediately jumped to $5.00 per acre. Jim tried to buy the land around the whole lake so that others would not fish on it, but did not quite manage.

Jim and Belle returned to Honolulu and Jim started fig-

Jim and friend

CHAPTER TWENTY-TWO

uring out how much it would all cost, and Belle's brother, architect Will Dickey designed a lodge. Confident that he could work out a deal, Jim paid the Cowans to move to the lake and began preliminary work on the lodge. A year later, Jim returned with Harry Mac-Conaughey and his youngest children, Charley and Barbara.

Jim thought there should be a membership of 50 individuals, to be paid for with a $1,000 membership fee, without dues. It would be called the Pennask Lake Company, Limited, and Mac-Conaughey was assigned to draft the articles of incorporation. 1,000 shares of $100 par value common stock were authorized.

The purpose of the corporation was, "To establish, maintain, and conduct a summer resort for the accommodation of members of the Company and their friends and to provide a hotel or chalet with boathouse, boats, and other conveniences and generally to afford to members and their friends all the accommodation and convenience of a summer resort for fishing, shooting and sporting purposes."

Of the $65,000, which was raised, Jim himself invested $50,000. The sixteen chartered member-investors were from Honolulu, San Francisco, New York, and British Columbia. Six were from Honolulu. At the date of incorporation of the Pennask Lake Club on November 1, 1929, members included a number of officers and directors of Hapco. Some of the subscribers, along with Jim Dole and H. E. MacConaughey, were J.H. Worrall, assistant secretary; A. G. Budge, director; and Frank C. Atherton, director. Frank Atherton was also the president and Alexander G. Budge was a vice president of Castle & Cooke. Only a few of them actually fished at Pennask Lake.

One of the founding members was John Hancock, a partner of Lehman Brothers, a New York investment banking firm. He was referred to at Lehman Brothers as a "corporate doctor," and served on the boards of directors of 22 companies.

Another of the founding members was John Kieckhefer. He had dropped out of high school to work at his father's wood box business, and assumed control of the company in 1915. In 1920, the company changed its name to Kieckhefer Container Company, and expanded to pulp and paper. His business expanded, and years later in the late 1950s he sold out to Weyerhaeuser.

The site of the log lodge was picked to maximize the view of the lake and the surrounding mountain and forests. When completed it had three stories, a large fireplace, a main hall, a dining room, and a "well equipped kitchen." There was a large wharf for mooring the boats, and a barn for horses. Twenty fish per day was set as the limit.

There are a number of islands within Pennask Lake. Jim named one of them "Belle Island." There were a couple of other small lakes in the vicinity : "Cowan Lake" and "Little Pennask."

The lodge was officially opened in the fall of 1929, with Mrs. Cowan as manager, assisted by her husband and by a hired hand, Philip. The first full season for the lodge was 1930. The Club was opened just in time for the Great Depression.

Boat mooring at the club

THE DEPRESSION HITS

Jim at his Honolulu office in the late 20's

In 1931, Hapco had been in business for thirty years. It had just spent $1.8 million to build a new four-story office building and to buy canning equipment to increase the capacity of the cannery, and over $6.0 million on Lanai, and it was processing more pineapple than ever. The company had all its land, production facilities, capital, and labor and management resources working together.

When the depression hit the mainland, Jim knew about it, but sales were moving along fairly well, and even though there was a seven percent drop in prices and profit margins were weak and earnings per share down 20 percent from the previous year, he did not think at first that his company would be affected. In 1930, the company generated sales of $12.2 million and earnings of $2.5 million, down only slightly from 1929 levels, despite higher capital costs due to added capacity. Hapco met the slack demand by extending national advertising to the radio. In the first half of 1930, MacConaughey, in San Francisco, kept wanting more cases of pineapple, especially the lower priced crushed pineapple, so plantings were continued instead of being curtailed.

In Hapco's 1931 Annual Stockholders' Report, Jim wrote that due to favorable weather and improved harvesting techniques, Hapco had had a record output of canned pineapple — 181,331 tons of fresh pineapple processed and 4.9 million cases packed. No longer was there a shortage of supply, and the company was geared up for strong product demand. Market share had been increased with its pack representing 38 percent of the total Hawaiian output.

Jim expected the company to have the best year it had ever had, and then the depression hit. Jim had faced economic downturns in 1909 and 1910, 1912, 1914, 1921, 1924 and 1927, but this time it was different. There had

CHAPTER TWENTY-THREE

been losses of $10,000 in 1903, and of $5,000 in 1904, but the 1931 loss was $3.9 million, or $5.20 per share for each of the 745,340 shares outstanding. Revenues had declined 40 percent. $2.4 million of the losses were associated with inventory markdowns due to lower prices, but the loss was far more severe than Jim had believed possible. By June 1932, Hapco was sitting with a total of $2.5 million of unsold cases of canned pineapple.

At first Jim was not too worried. The company maintained its contributions to the company's retirement plan and paid its cash dividend in the third quarter of the year. Jim reported to the board of directors: "This depression was at first expected by nearly everyone to be short lived. Although sales fell off, occasional spurts, together with false starts in the general situation, gave promise of an early bettering of conditions."

Jim considered his most serious mistake in the crisis was in failing to move quickly enough to adjust prices to market conditions. He avoided cutting prices at first in order to maintain the company's integrity with the Association of Pineapple Canners.

The peach canners in California were the first to cut prices. They were in better shape to cut prices than Hapco, because they bought fresh peaches from independent farmers and could pass some of the losses back to the farmers. Not so for Hapco and the other fully integrated Hawaii pineapple producers.

A few months into the year, Hapco did slash prices by about 25 percent, but MacConaughey was slow in carrying out the price cuts. When the situation continued to worsen, although the board of directors resisted it, prices were cut another 35 percent. The price cuts did help move the pineapples, but not enough.

Jim was fearful that wholesalers would not pass the price cuts on to the consumers, trying to protect their margins, so he offered to absorb the losses suffered because of low prices by giving rebates to the distributors for their "floor stocks." These losses showed up in Hapco's 1931 financial reports.

The company also cut down its expenses for 1932 nearly 60 percent from the prior year by processing fewer fruit. In 1931, 181,000 tons were processed and in 1932, only 34,300 tons of the 200,000 tons of ripe pineapple in the ground was harvested.

The company responded as it had so many times before to downturns by trying to stimulate sales through increased advertising, but it did not make drastic cuts immediately in expenses. The increased advertising helped a little, but the effort was insufficient.

Jim tried to remain optimistic. He thought that the industry could be profitable, even in the depression, with about 35 percent less production than it had. With overproduction of about 50 percent, he advised his board of directors that given reasonable patience the condition of overproduction could be cured.

New ideas had helped before in hard times, and now Jim again tried to promote a new idea, this time pineapple juice. He had believed from the earliest days of Hapco's history, before the Wahiawa cannery was built, that it was possible to market unsweetened pineapple juice. One of the early Wahiawa pioneers, Thomas L. Halloway, who grew pineapple on his Wahiawa homestead located on the south side of Eames's homestead, had extracted the juice and sold it in a booth in Honolulu, and it had sold well. The cost of canning juice would be less than in canning sliced pineapple because there was no need to add sugar and there would be much less labor without all the workers at the trimming tables.

Jim's first pineapple juice venture was in 1910. There was demand for it, but

Hapco spent $1.8 million in 1931 on a new four story office building and canning equipment

the juice lost its quality when it came in contact with metal. Also the pineapple cells are hair cells, and tended to wrap around the cutting machines. That problem was finally solved by engineers Botley and Hoyt, in Hapco's production department, when they mixed coarse quartz sand with the ground pulp before it was pressed. This cut the hair cells and released the juice.

Pineapple juice was finally perfected when the depression began. The capacity for juice was there. If Hapco could recover only half of the lost juice, it could produce 75 million cases. Jim started a major marketing program that, is successful, would have pulled the company out of its troubles.

Jim was aware of a large market for canned liquids. The best selling item was canned milk, which at the time was 12.5 million tons annually, equivalent to 925 million cases of Hapco's #2 tall cans of pineapple. The beer industry, at the same time, was marketing 120 million cases of beer annually. Until mid-1932, little canned juice was being sold on the market. However, juices already on the market weren't going well. Tomato juice did well at first, but lost its popularity when fresh tomatoes became more available. Canned orange juice was not being

successfully marketed, and only 700,000 cases of grapefruit were sold a year. Still, Jim projected that given the market for canned liquids, Hapco could easily market 4.5 million cases of juice per year.

The biggest resistance to marketing pineapple juice came from Harry Mac-Conaughey, who had made up his mind that pineapple juice could not be sold in quantity, and at first the idea of selling pineapple juice didn't get beyond Hapco's board.

One problem in creating a market for pineapple juice was how to open the cans. Can openers then on the market required the removal of the entire top of the can. Jim personally wrote the American Can Company in mid-1932, suggesting that they find a better way to open cans, and it invented the "punch" can opener, still the most common bottle opener today, which was immediately put to use in the beer industry.

By August 1932, Hapco did sell 7,000 cases of juice, and for the entire year, it sold 134,260 cases.

The big problem was having enough money. At the end of 1930, Hapco had $7.3 million of working capital, but at the end of 1931 there was only $2.1 million, which wasn't enough to operate. This time the company raised $5.0 million in five year five percent gold notes, although Jim looked at the issuance of the five year note as an error and thought at the time, that the company could have arranged a better deal.

The following year, he wrote to Hapco's board, "It is a mystery how this got by any of us and it is clear that these notes approach closer and closer to the time when they will be current liabilities, which forms one of the serious complications in our financial problem and is recognized by the banks as being a menace to the advances which they make to us for our current operations." Jim advised the board in mid-1932 that if

CHAPTER TWENTY-THREE

In 1932, only 34,000 tons were processed

the company could return to profitability before the notes matured, even at materially lower production levels, it would be highly likely that with improved monetary conditions, the notes could be refunded. Another option would be to raise funds to purchase the notes at discounted prices.

Besides the gold notes, the company had $4.5 million of bank loans due in less than a year, up from $1.8 million the prior year.

Jim's recommendation to the board in mid-1932 was that if the bankers, which included the Guarantee Trust Company and the Bank of Hawaii, among others, were still uncomfortable with the company's efforts to climb out of its financial crisis, Hapco could raise another 500,000 shares via a rights offering to existing stockholders, perhaps by means of monthly assessments. Any stock not accepted by existing stockholders could be offered to mainland customers and/or suppliers. At the end of 1931, Hapco had 745,340 shares outstanding. A 500,000 rights offering would increase outstanding stock by over 65 percent. There would be no dilution if existing stockholders bought the newly issued stock.

A second choice Dole recommended to his board was to issue enough new shares of convertible preferred stock to call and retire the five year gold notes, the offering to be in the form of a preemptive rights offering to existing stockholders on a pro-rata basis.

The advantage of both of these approaches, Jim explained to the board, was to have more of the stock in the hands of the Hawaiian based stockholders. "There would be the advantage of having perhaps the entire Hawaiian financial group interested in and behind the company, and this might have very far reaching effects during future years."

Should additional equity financing not be available in Hawaii, Jim thought the money could be raised on the mainland. While the company couldn't have picked a worse time to try to attract new stockholders, Frank Weld of White Weld & Company, a New York Investment Banker, approached Jim on this. Furthermore, John Hancock, partner at Lehman Brothers and co-stockholder with Jim at the Pennask Lake Company, Limited, offered his efforts in facilitating a Hapco financing.

Another possibility, noted Jim, was selling out to General Foods. General Foods first approached Hapco in 1929 and again in 1931 about an acquisition. Canned pineapple was apparently a good fit with General Foods' massive distribution network. Furthermore, General Foods was interested in acquiring all of the Hawaii pineapple companies and handling all processed pineapple output from a single selling office in Honolulu.

Another option would be to sell Hapco's assets to C.P.C. Jim thought Hapco's board should seriously consider some type of a combination with C.P.C., even though a merger between the two, valued at $46.7 million, had previously been turned down by Hapco. Jim thought that C.P.C. was in much better financial shape than Hapco.

Another alternative solution would be to form an agricultural credit corporation and secure funds from the Reconstruction Finance Corporation.

Any of the above efforts might have solved its financial problems.

REORGANIZATION

Despite Jim's continued optimism, Hapco's condition worsened over the course of the 1932 year, and none of the possibilities worked out. The pineapple industry was hit worse than any other part of Hawaii's economy, so the bad times in Hawaii were blamed on Jim. Now, instead of being idolized, he became the scapegoat.

The 1932 Report to Stockholders' letter to stockholders was signed by John Whitmore, vice president, and not by Jim. Whitmore told about the company's "drastic retrenchment," after its revenues had fallen from $7.2 million in 1931 to $6.1 million in 1932, with a loss to the company of $8.4 million in 1932. Included in the loss were asset write-downs of pineapple not harvested and inventories of $5.1 million. The company had cut production of pineapple from 181,331 tons in 1931

Students worked at cannery during summer vacation

to 34,331 tons in 1932. It had cut salaries, and had cut its contributions to the retirement system from $131,000 in 1931 to $1,988 in 1932. 2,500 acres had also been sold to C.P.C.

The company's financial condition was not healthy, but of the $12.3 million of losses incurred in 1931 and 1932, $7.5 million were from asset write-downs and only $4.8 million was from operations. Even including the $12.3 million losses in the latest two years and the losses in the first two years it was in business, Hapco had earned $13.5 mil-

lion over the 30 years it was in business. Stockholders' equity as of December 31, 1932, prior to the reorganization was $8.3 million. The company was not bankrupt.

But the bankers had Hapco in a bind. In Hawaii at that time there was a group of sugar agents that was called "The Big Five," American Factors, Alexander and Baldwin, Theo. Davies and Co., C. Brewer, and Castle and Cooke, and it controlled most of the sugar crop and every business associated with sugar, including the banks. It was intertwined with interlocking directorships with each other and with the banks. While Jim served on the board of the National Canners Association and the Association of Hawaiian Pineapple Canners, he was not on the board of the Bank of Hawaii or any of the "Big Five" sugar companies, so he lacked the corporate sponsorship.

Jim had already enraged the Big Five earlier by taking Hapco's freight business away from Matson and giving it to another company, Isthmian Lines, which offered a lower rate. With Waialua Agriculture's interest in Hapco, Hapco's board was peppered with Big Five members, who were not sympathetic to Jim. The banks told Jim that they would lend the company the money it needed only if he stepped down from the position of president and chief executive officer. He was told that it would be impossible for the company to raise the money on the mainland, and there was no money available locally. He was discouraged by now and perhaps the strain was too much for him, and he had one of his spells of depression. At any rate, he gave up and, in order to save the company, agreed to the terms.

Equity financing was also needed. On November 15, 1932, Waialua Agriculture proposed a reorganization of Hawaiian Pine, which was accepted by the board and completed on December 29, 1932. A new corporation was formed which would assume the debt of Hapco. This debt included the $3.0 million of bank loans, which the company had borrowed to build its new office building and renovated cannery, plus the $5.0 million of gold notes due in 1936.

A new company was to be created which would carry the same name as the old one, with $1.5 million of convertible preferred stock underwritten by Waialua Agriculture Company and Castle & Cooke. Each share of convertible preferred stock was entitled to four votes,

while each share of common stock was entitled to one vote. Also, 2.0 million shares of common stock were authorized for the new company. Stockholders of the old company in consideration for their 747,211 shares surrendered, received 500,000 shares of $5.00 par value common stock of the new company. Hapco stockholders, who could have sold out to C.P.C. a few years prior for $46.7 million, were now exchanging their shares for $2.5 million worth of stock in the new company. Included in the terms of the new financing was a condition that the stock held by the present common stockholders of the corporation would be held in an escrow account until the debt of the corporation was paid off. Jim was to step down as president and Atherton Richards, treasurer of Castle & Cooke, was to be elected president and chief executive officer of the new Hapco.

The mastermind of the recapitalization was Castle & Cooke. Castle & Cooke owned only 1.2 percent of Hapco stock prior to the reorganization, but it owned 22 percent of Waialua Agriculture, which was the largest single stockholder of Hapco, owning 33.4 percent of all of Hapco's outstanding common stock. Castle & Cooke was controlled by the S.N. Castle Estate, Limited, which owned 27.5 percent, and the J. B. Atherton Estate, Limited which owned 31 percent of the stock. The J.B. Atherton Estate, Limited, was a family holding corporation held by or in trust for the descendants of J. B. Atherton. Among the descendants were Frank C. Atherton and Atherton Richards. Frank Atherton was the president of Castle & Cooke, and also a director of Waialua Agriculture Co. Atherton Richards was Castle and Cooke's treasurer. Through the reorganization of Hapco, which included stock options to buy Hapco's common stock at $6.00 per share, Waialua and Castle & Cooke together acquired 57

percent of the outstanding voting stock of Hapco.

Waialua Agriculture was Hapco's largest stockholder prior to the reorganization. No other stockholder owned more than 5 percent. It is not known by this writer what Hunt did with his stock, or how much stock Jim Dole owned. However, Waialua did not have the financial resources to subscribe on a pro rata basis to any new stock offered. Castle & Cooke did and was willing to underwrite a new issue of stock providing that it had sufficient stock options to acquire control of Hapco and have its own management team in place in the company and would thereby be Hapco's agent. Waialua Agriculture had the support of the banks and the votes among Hapco's stockholders to accomplish its objectives.

Jim was "promoted" to the newly created position of Chairman of the Board, and was advised by the Board to "take a long vacation..." His position was a place of stature with no voice in the management of the affairs of the company. Dole's voice could be heard only by his vote in proportion to the few shares he owned.

As to whether Jim could have blocked the reorganization by means of a proxy fight, it is unlikely, according to Deane W. Malott, Hapco vice president and close associate of Jim's during the reorganization. Deane was the Assistant Dean teaching at Harvard Business School when Jim recruited him in 1929 under a one-year contract specifically to survey Hapco and its position in the industry, but he remained with the firm as vice president until 1933. He stood by Jim during his troubles and was a lifelong friend. Deane said that Jim had the support of his employees, who owned quite a lot of stock and could have supported him in a proxy fight, and that with employee-stockholder votes in his favor, he might have put up a good fight, but he probably would still have lost. Malott thought that if Jim had not agreed to relinquish his position as president and general manager, the Board would have fired him.

CHAPTER TWENTY-FOUR

JIM AFTER HAPCO

The house on Green Street

Jim's salary at Hapco peaked in 1925 at $50,000 per year. It was scaled down significantly in 1932, and finally, in the reorganization, cut to $15,000. The arrangement with the new Hapco was to pay Jim a salary for life starting with the $15,000 but in an amount based on a formula depending on Hapco's profits, assuming that he would be available as a consultant if Hapco wanted him. After the depression, it went up to $20,000, then $30,000 a year.

For thirty years Jim had his heart and soul in his pineapple company. What a wrench it must have been for him to give up control of its operations.

It was not only a heart-breaking time for Jim but a tough time for him financially. He had put all his efforts into Hapco, and now all that was left of that was the official title of chairman of the board without a management voice, his

$15,000 a year and an interest in Hapco stock that was eventually scaled back to about 100 shares. He was at least partially supporting his oldest son, Dick. Jimmy had dropped out of college, but might go back. Betty was at Vassar. Charley and Barbara were still at Punahou and would soon be entering college. Besides, Belle was accustomed to a certain standard of living. There were also the Pennask Lake Club expenses.

Jim started selling his property in Hawaii. Hapco's vice president and secretary, Kenneth Barnes, and MacConaughey helped him do it. They worked with a number of real estate brokers, but there were no immediate offers. He was forced to take the best prices available. The Green Street home sold, finally, for about $25,000. (The owners later subdivided the land into lots. The house remained for a while, but was later torn down and apartment buildings put up in its place. There is no sign of it left today.)

Jim owned some real estate in the heart of Seattle, which he let go for taxes. He owned land on the windward side of Oahu jointly with Harold Castle, and gave that up. Gone was the house on Kahala beach and the lot on Kailua beach. The only Hawaii real estate he did not sell was the original Wahiawa homestead.

After his "vacation," Jim contacted Atherton Richards in Honolulu who informed him that he would not be needed at the company for the present and encouraged him to extend his vacation.

Richards did suggest to Jim, however, that he meet with the executive committee of the U.S. Government's Food Industries Advisory Board. On the committee were CEO's of Proctor & Gamble, General Foods, and other major companies in the food-related industry. This led to five months in Washington, D.C. where Jim served as the Chief of the Food Products Section, Division of Processing and Marketing, the Agricultural Adjustment Administration (AAA) for purposes of drawing up food codes. Jim was amused to later recollect that what with the red tape there, he never managed to issue a single code for food products.

After leaving Washington, Jim moved to San Francisco, where he and Belle lived for several years in the Gaylord Hotel before buying an apartment on Union Street with a spectacular view of the bay.

Jim had been disillusioned in Honolulu by men whom he had considered his friends, but in San Francisco, Jake Blumlein turned out to be a true friend, as loyal in hard times as in good. Jim had many talks with him. Jake gave him pep talks, told him that now that he was no longer on top of the world, he should be more careful how he dressed. Jake probably pointed out to him that he still had a lot going for him, his contacts, his experience and his know how. It was probably Jake, more than anyone else, who helped Jim to accept the situation and to pick himself up and go on. At any rate, Jim was soon full of ideas and eager to pursue them.

Unhappy with the "New Deal," Jim thought that with the U.S. off the gold standard there was certain to be runaway inflation, and gold would become increasingly valuable, so gold dredging was the first thing he went into. He started out by looking for gold mines in British Columbia, near Pennask Lake, and in the California river-beds.

His first success was with the Arroyo Seco Gold Dredging Company, which had a successful tract in Ione, California. Jim got his money back in one year, and the mine produced gold for several years and brought in more with the eventual sale of the dredge. Jim gave each of his children stock in Arroyo Seco, and they received dividends every month until the gold gave out. Charley's took care of his expenses at the Harvard Business School, and Betty's dividends helped in her early married days on Kauai and in Honolulu.

After a few more gold tries, Jim formed James D. Dole & Associates on December 1, 1937, with three partners, James Sharpe, Alexis Post and Alexander Donald. It was a San Francisco-based venture capital general partnership formed to investigate business opportunities, patents and inventions to develop into business enterprises.

Jim turned over all his gold projects to the partnership. After Arroyo Seco, they hadn't gone well. His comments about his gold exploration activities as a whole are summarized as follows: "While they included some very successful developments, on the whole too much money was spent with unfavorable re-

Jim and his Hapco Chairman retirement gift in 1948

sults to warrant the indefinite continuation of the business."

Alexis Post's father was a Czarist Colonel who had defected from Russia and arrived in Oakland just after the 1906 earthquake. Post had graduated from Stanford in 1922 with honors in mechanical engineering. He had been with Standard Oil of California and West Coast lumber operations before joining the partnership.

James Sharpe had also graduated from Stanford with a degree in electrical engineering, and had then received an MBA from Harvard. He was with General Motors before joining with Jim.

Alexander Donald was a graduate of Harvard and previously was a professor at Harvard Business School.

Harry Goff later joined the partnership as an assistant manager in January, 1946. He had graduated from Stanford in 1937 and Harvard Business School in 1939. He was with National Lead Co. in San Francisco for two years and then had served during World War II as a Lt. Commander in the Navy on the battleship Wisconsin in the Pacific. He decided not to return to National Lead Co. and became interested in working with Jim when he was told that Jim was an entrepreneur noted for integrity and honesty who knew many people and had put together a series of companies subsequent to returning from his stint in Washington. A portrait of Jim Dole still hangs in Goff's office.

Goff, reminiscing later, said that Jim would sit in the lounge at the Pacific Union Club on Nob Hill and discuss ventures with the people there who respected him, and that he would raise money for corporate ideas in increments of $10,000 each. Jim would tell the people that he had his own money in these deals, and that "If the whole thing goes down the drain, you can still have a drink with me at the bar."

In time, as the investee companies grew, it was determined that they could no longer be operated as a group. Each would have to be able to "stand alone." Each of the partners was to take over the operation of one of the companies. Sharpe and Donald then withdrew from the partnership. The others continued, Jim with a 40 percent interest in the partnership, Post with 35 percent, and Goff with 25 percent. Not all the ventures were successful, but three, especially, were.

In the engineering field, Jim Dole was intrigued with a device developed by Henry Schwartz. This was a comminutor extractor, or pulverizer for food products. The engineering company could build the machine, but it needed an end user. S&W fit that bill. Schwartz Engineering and S&W formed a joint venture. The firm was first named Schwartz Engineering Co., then James Dole Engineering Company until one of the directors commented that the company was not really an engineering company and the name was changed to James Dole Corporation. Initially, about 1/3 of the stock was owned by James D. Dole & Associates. James Dole & Associates had operating control of Schwartz, although the company had some 2,000 shareholders.

Unfiltered apple juice, once pasteurized, turns brown almost immediately because of oxidation. Jim found a scientist named Dr. William McKinley Martin who previously had developed an instrument for measuring the degree of cooking in processed peas for the American Can Company. Jim Dole hired him, and he developed a de-aerator, a device that removes oxygen from food products by centrifugal motion. This device separated the pulp from the liquid in a vacuum when pasteurized so that it was not subject to subsequent oxidation and the liquid apple juice stayed white. S&W used this machine to introduce "liquid apple" juice, which was understood to be the first unfiltered apple juice on the

Jim and Belle on vacation

market. The joint venture was called Comminuted Foods. The device was manufactured and used by S&W, which distributed the "Liquid Apple" in cans and bottles. While filtered apple juice still outsells unfiltered apple juice by a margin of three-to-one, unfiltered apple juice is a top apple juice seller in health food stores. The device was also sold to other users. A plant to manufacture liquid apple was constructed on S&W property until the company's own plant could be constructed.

Another success was with aseptic canning. In 1946 Dr. Martin developed a major innovation in food processing. This was aseptic canning. Sterilization of low acid food products in canning had always been accomplished by utilizing various forms of pressure retort where the food was sterilized in containers. Along with the growth of markets for processed foods, there were growing requirements for the treatment of heat sensitive foods, large container packaging and new types of food packages. Aseptic canning departed from in-container sterilization of foods by a method whereby food products pre-sterilized by high temperature-short time methods could be filled and seamed under sterile conditions, using pre-sterilized containers and lids, all in a high speed continuous operation. Super-heated steam constituted a dry gas that sterilized the containers. In other words, pre-sterilized food products would be pumped to the sterile containers by means of double tubular or other heat-exchangers.

Aseptic canning allows the process of sterilization to be accomplished at high temperatures over a significantly shorter period of time than the normal canning process, and with less destruction of vitamins, color and food quality. This was a breakthrough in food processing, and Jim thought that aseptic canning could revolutionize the whole concept of food processing. Aseptic canning principles have been utilized widely to produce products such as concentrated milk, and have been applied on various sizes and types of containers. Although the James Dole Corporation is noted for other things, it is most noted for its development of aseptic canning.

Discussing old times with Ah Woa

Chemical Process Company was a developer of resinous ion exchangers which utilized the "Duolite" trademark. Chemical Process was in the anion and cation fields. A cation yields a positive charge that attracts a minus electron to neutralize something. Anion yields a negative charge that attracts a plus electron to make zero or neutralize. The cation exchangers are for de-mineralization, water purification, etc. Dow Chemical was a major competitor, but Chemical Process was still a participant. The anion exchangers are highly selective. Jim Dole thought that they could be used for the removal of selective ions so that sugar could be refined by the use of ion-exchangers. They have not been used in sugar refining but are used in the processing of various foodstuffs including syrups. James D. Dole & Associates owned about a third of the outstanding stock of Chemical Process Company.

Aluviones Selectos was one of the more successful gold dredging ventures of the partnership. This company had a large dredge on the Patia River near Popayon, Columbia. The company had 700 employees. However, since Jim couldn't trust the absentee management which were mining the gold, he decided to get rid of it. The partnership sold Aluviones Selectos to Newmont Mining in 1949 for $3 million. The primary asset of the company was a lease from the Columbia government and the dredge. About 300,000 to 400,000 ounces of gold were dredged each year which was sent to China via Macao and sold at a premium price. The partnership owned about a third interest in Aluviones Selectos.

James D. Dole & Associates continued until Jim Dole's retirement in 1954. Upon his retirement, Jim was paid $50,000 in cash as a deduction from the interest in the respective shares of stock held and in shares of the investee companies, and the name of the partnership

View from their apartment in San Francisco

was changed to Post/Goff & Associates. Some of the partnership holdings went on to be very successful in later years.

In 1981, James D. Dole Corp. (formerly James Dole Engineering) was merged into Newport Corp., located in Newport Beach, with the name and business activities of James Dole Corp. sold to its employees and a few outside investors close to the company. The employee management and investor group then sold the Aseptic Canning rights to Graham Engineering of York, Pa. The Dole name was changed to JDC Manufacturing, Inc., which operates as a sophisticated job shop in the company's original premises in Redwood City, California. Under a contract with Graham Engineering, JDC Manufacturing, Inc. continues to manufacture all of the aseptic canning equipment sold by Graham Engineering and provides technical service.

The merger gained Newport about 2,000 stockholders to its original 15. James Dole Corp. needed the earnings of Newport, and Newport needed James Dole Corp.'s shareholders. Newport is a leader in laser optics and vibration isolated tables used to deaden vibration in a sensitive laboratory environment. Initially, about a third of the stock was owned by James Dole & Associates. Less was held at the time of the merger. At the time of Jim Dole's retirement, the Newport stock sold under $5 per share. Now, in the 1980's it is publicly traded on NASDAQ (National Association of Security Dealers Automated Quotations) at about $15 per share after three stock splits, with 9.4 million shares outstanding.

By the time Jim Dole retired, Chemical Process was doing well. On August 15, 1961 it was merged for about $13 per share with Diamond Alkali (Diamond Alkali later changed its name to Diamond Shamrock). In 1961 Chemical Process Company had 766,650 shares outstanding.

The James Dole Corp. and Chemical Process were most successful after Jim Dole retired, but, as Harry Goff has said, Jim deserves much of the credit for initiating them and maintaining their survival during some very trying times.

CHAPTER TWENTY-FIVE

DOLE FOODS

Strong customer acceptance around the world

A few months after Jim resigned as president and general manager of Hapco, John Whitmore died. Another victim of the depression was Phil Tucker. It is understood that the stock market crash of 1929 and the resulting depression took all that he had.

The depression eventually ended. Hapco survived and prospered and became Castle & Cooke's largest subsidiary. With fresh money in the company, the advertising that Jim had been planning and the promotion of pineapple juice were put into effect. "DOLE" as the trademark or brand name was finally used for the first time.

Prices per processed ton were slow to recover. The price per ton had been $178.50 in 1920. In 1930 the price went down to $114.38, and dropped during the depression to a low of $56.60. By 1942 to 1943, the price per ton rose, but only to $107.03. (These prices compare with an estimated $400 per ton in 1987.) Pineapple processing, however, reached a new record in the 1935 to 1936 year of over 200,000 tons.

One reason for the lower price per ton of processed pineapple was competition that held price increases well below the rate of inflation. Another reason was a shift from sliced pineapple to pineapple juice. Juice did not bring as high a price per case as sliced fruit. 695,623 cases of juice were packed in 1934 and 4.5 million cases in 1935, over 30 percent of the entire pack.

In 1961, three years after Jim Dole's death, Hapco was merged into Castle & Cooke, and became Dole Pineapple Company, a wholly owned subsidiary. Dole Pineapple Co. was subsequently changed to Dole Foods Company. Only after his death was the Dole name used as a corporate name.

Other parts of the world began to be more and more competitive, in large part because of rising labor costs in Hawaii. Dole Foods participated in this competition by shifting much of its pineapple activities abroad. In 1930, the bulk of all the canned pineapple in the world was produced in Hawaii. By 1985, Hawaii's share of the world market declined to 17 percent.

It is doubtful that even if Jim Dole had remained in the pineapple industry he could have done anything about the foreign competition. Harry Goff, who had been associated with Jim for a long time, felt that had Jim Dole remained as president and general manager of Hapco beyond 1932, he could not have changed Hapco's fortunes. He could not have done much in regard to the stiff foreign competition and he probably would not have been able to do much about the organization of labor into unions. The cost of labor went up during World War II. It went up even more after Harry Bridges unionized the Filipino work force in Hawaii, and the cost of labor became too great to increase pineapple production in Hawaii.

Castle & Cooke expanded into a number of businesses other than pineapple and sugar, such as canned tuna, salmon and crab, and began to sell fresh fruit, such as bananas and pineapple and also fresh vegetables. It also started to develop its vast real estate holdings

The largest processor and distributor of fresh food products in the world

through its wholly-owned subsidiary, Oceanic Properties.

In the early-to-mid 1980's, Castle & Cooke got into financial trouble itself, because of the competition and bad weather. It lost $50 million in 1983 and $77 million in 1984. The 1983 loss included a $58 million pretax special charge, relating mostly to the costs of restructuring the company's banana production and distribution systems and the costs of relocating personnel. The losses included discontinued operations of $18 million in 1983 and $78 million in 1984. By March 23, 1985, Castle & Cooke's balance sheet had deteriorated to the point where its stockholders' equity was less than $295 million (including $96 million of preferred stock) compared with short-term debt of $118 million and long-term debt of $373 million.

Not surprisingly, Castle & Cooke, like Hapco, began to have trouble with its bankers. Long term debt included a $70 million revolving line of credit with a consortium of European banks, terminating on June 30, 1985, and a $80 million revolving line of credit with a consortium of U.S. banks, terminating on December 15, 1986. By June 16, 1984, Castle & Cooke had borrowed $105 million on these lines. The company also had $186 million of sinking fund requirements on long term debt due in 1986. It was in a liquidity squeeze. It was unable to pay $97 million of principal payments due its lenders and could not renew $50 million of commercial paper. Because of restrictions in bank loan agreements, it was also unable to pay interest on its publicly traded 5-3/8 percent convertible subordinated debentures due in 1994 and 12 percent subordinated notes due in 1991. Peat, Marwick, Mitchell & Co., the company's auditors, in its opinion on Castle & Cooke's 1984 financial statements, said it was questionable as to whether the firm had the financial capacity "...to continue as a going concern." The company blamed its misfortune on the weather and ornery competitors.

Celebreties such as Kenny Rogers are used to promote the Dole name

Castle & Cooke was able to restructure its debt only by merging with Flexi-Van, a New York based transportation equipment leasing company, effective July 1, 1985. As a result of the merger, Flexi-Van stockholders ended up owning approximately 51 percent of Castle & Cooke, if they exercised their stock options. The principal stockholder of Flexi-Van was David H. Murdock, who owned 34 percent of the common stock. Murdock became Castle & Cooke's new chairman of the board, president and chief executive officer.

Profits of the consolidated company subsequently recovered and certain assets of Flexi-Van were sold. In 1987, Castle & Cooke divested its remaining Flexi-Van interests via a rights offering to stockholders and Flexi-Van later went private.

Castle & Cooke was left with Dole Foods and Oceanic Properties, and it continues as a food and real estate holding company. Through the 1985 merger with Flexi-Van and open market purchases, Murdock became the largest single stockholder of Castle & Cooke, owning 25 percent of the outstanding capital stock of Castle & Cooke according to the April 11, 1988 proxy statement.

Dole Foods Company operates as a unit of Castle & Cooke's food group, with pineapple produced all over the world. Castle & Cooke today has over 40,000 employees, operates in 50 countries and does over $2 billion in business. It is the largest processor and distributor of fresh food products in the world. Included are more than 30 fruits, vegetables and nuts. No longer involved in seafood, the company distributes pineapples, bananas, lettuce, celery, tomatoes, citrus fruits, cauliflower, broccoli, carrots, strawberries, table grapes, melons, coconuts, bell peppers, raisins, avocados, almonds, pistachios, plums, cherries, and dates. It distributes roughly

7 percent of all the produce consumed in the U.S. market today, and over 30 percent of all the produce found in U.S. grocery stores. The company is the largest producer and marketer of pineapple in the world with a 40 percent market share in the U.S. As for Castle & Cooke's global food plan, the major thrust seems to be in fresh fruit. Of total Dole Foods' sales of $2.0 billion, only $500 million came from packaged foods (including canned pineapple). According to David Murdock, Dole Foods intends to increase further its global scope.

After using the DOLE name with pineapple, Castle & Cooke began to use it with favorable successes on more and more of its products, such as bananas, other fruit and fresh vegetables. Consumers are believed to like the DOLE brand as much as other well known consumer products. DOLE is an easy name to remember and is a name associated with premium quality. Studies that the company has done indicate that people find the DOLE brand one that they can trust as "a good wholesome product." Dole Foods senior vice president, Chuck Bauman, thinks that the DOLE brand name "will outdistance any other processed canned product."

In the Japanese markets, the company markets fresh kiwi's, lemons and oranges under the DOLE label. The DOLE brand has also been transferred to fresh vegetables. DOLE's new dried fruit & nut division has also found wide consumer acceptance under the DOLE franchise for raisins, dates, almonds and pistachios.

Dole Foods found through marketing studies that the Dole name could be extended to other fruits and natural "health related" products in the U.S. market, so the company has used it with products that may or may not have

The popular show draws crowds at The Cannery

CHAPTER TWENTY-SIX

pineapple in them. It has used it with frozen desserts, fruit bars, refrigerated and frozen juices, dry fruit and nuts. As a result of acquiring fruit and nut companies, the company has found that because these products are natural, the DOLE brand name has been extendable to them. This is consistent with the "bursting sun" logo associated with the DOLE brand name because it reflects that the products are grown in the sun.

Dole Foods has considerable competitive strength in the food industry, and is in a good position to extend the DOLE brand franchise into a number of food products, either internally or by acquisition. Based on size, Dole Foods and Del Monte are about even with $2.0 to $2.5 billion in sales; Beatrice/Hunt-Wesson does $3 billion, subsequent to the acquisition by Beatrice; Tri/Valley, which owns S&W, with $.7 billion.

Dole Foods processes pineapple in three countries today. Dole Thailand packs 200,000 tons of fruit per year, Dole Philippines packs 380,000 tons, and Dole Hawaii packs 225,000 tons. The distribution of the market share in the U.S. retail markets for canned pineapple is as follows: Dole (48%), Del Monte (14%), Private Label (30%), and Third Tier (8%). The Third Tier pineapple includes pineapple produced by Dole, Del Monte, Maui Pine and Thailand pineapple. The largest in the private label area is Maui Pine.

As for its position in Hawaii, Murdock feels that with the cost of labor at $100 a day in Hawaii, compared with $3.50 in Thailand and $7.50 in the Philippines, it is hard to compete in agriculture with other regions of the world, especially since the quality of Hawaiian pineapple is no longer much better than pineapple grown elsewhere. The pineapple from the Philippines is almost as good.

Productivity is the only thing that will help Hawaiian pineapple to survive. "If we weren't productive, we would have been out of business long ago," said Dole plantation manager, Jim Parker. Hawaii's cost of labor is partially offset by production efficiencies so that there are higher yields per acre. The total plantation costs are about the same in Hawaii as in the Philippines, but the Hawaii costs accelerate with the labor needed for harvesting the fruit and handling it in the cannery.

Murdock thinks that Hawaii's high costs of output can only be offset by the production of higher margin agricultural products which can be marketed through Hawaii's visitor industry. He expressed a willingness to commit funds to achieve this purpose.

Since air transportation has speeded up the delivery of fresh pineapple to the supermarkets on the mainland, and there is less labor involved when the pineapples are sold as fresh fruit, the fresh fruit operation has become very profitable. As many of the pineapples as possible which are grown at Wahiawa are sold as fresh fruit. There are about 7,500 acres of pineapple in Wahiawa, which yield about 150,000 tons of pineapple per year. The pineapples which aren't satisfactory for the fresh fruit market, about half of them, are sent to the cannery.

The pineapples from Lanai are barged right into the cannery, and all of them are canned. The total Lanai tonnage for 1989 is estimated at 180,000 tons, of which 50,000 will be in the summer and the rest spread throughout the year. The Lanai plantation has a gross acreage of 16,000, not counting all the roads and other land that can't be utilized. 9,000 acres are now in production on Lanai as compared to Jim Dole's objective of 20,000.

The land under the cannery in downtown Honolulu is valuable, so the cannery is being streamlined to get it within 25 acres, which will leave 30 acres free to

The Dole name has been extended to other fruits and natural "health related" products in the U.S. market

be used for other commercial purposes. The main office building in the cannery has been converted into a tourist attraction with cannery tours and gift shops. Also in the building are the offices for Oceanic Leisure, a unit of Oceanic Properties. The operating group for the cannery is going to move from the fourth floor into an adjacent building.

This renovation is being brought about by a $21 million program. All the construction is of modern, stainless steel. Some of the old and outdated equipment are museum pieces that will be refurbished and shown in the museum. This has been going on while the cannery has continued to operate. "We are building a cannery right in the middle of an operating cannery," said Bob Hawthorne, vice president and general manager of Dole Packaged Foods Company, Hawaii Division.

Included in the modernization program is a new fresh fruit packing station in Wahiawa where a "modern, state of the art" operation may be developed.

The goal of the program is to find a comfortable, stable production level which will balance with the company's fresh pineapple operations. In spite of the streamlining, the company will continue to pack 220,000 to 250,000 tons of fruit annually at the cannery, compared with the 180,000 Hapco processed in 1931.

Canned pineapple makes up about 50 percent of the company's processed food sales today, with the other 50 percent in refrigerated and frozen juices and blended juices. Sales of juices and juice blends have increased substantially in recent years because of their good profit margins. According to Doug Jocelin, vice president, International Dole Foods, gross margins for canned pineapple is 33 percent today. Gross margins for refrigerated juices is about 36 percent, and frozen and blended juices about 37 percent. The company has also branched out into other things such as frozen desserts, which may have no connection to pineapple other than its fruit base.

CHAPTER TWENTY-SIX

A wide variety of Dole products are available at The Cannery

Dole Foods believes that there is more opportunity for juice blends than for canned pineapple today, because life styles have changed. Consumers are looking for more beverages, and more juices will be sold in vending machines and/or refrigerators as opposed to soft drinks. The major increase is in juices other than orange juice and apple juice, according to senior vice president, Chuck Bauman. Pineapple juice is one of the better juices because it blends well with other juices. "It gives other juices a body without masking the flavor," he said.

People are also looking for foods they don't have to spend time preparing, Bauman said. "The challenge is that as the trend goes more and more toward convenience foods, whatever forms they take, pineapple continues to be a part of those trends."

The architect of the Castle & Cooke acquisition was David H. Murdock, who is chairman of the board and chief executive officer of Castle & Cooke, Flexi-Van, and a number of other corporations. Many viewed him as a corporate raider with intentions of selling Dole Foods to the highest bidder. Instead, he appears to have captured the spirit of the

Dole legacy and may be successful in marketing the DOLE brand name in existing and new value added products. Associated with agricultural products, Murdock intends to carry the DOLE brand name into non-agricultural products to sell to the visitor industry. Included are DOLE hats, DOLE t-shirts, and DOLE coffee mugs.

Something for everyone

WHAT HAPPENED TO PENNASK LAKE

The depression also had its effect on the Pennask Lake Club. It, too, started hurting for money. Some might have come in from the sale of new memberships in the Club which required approval of a membership committee and the purchase of 10 shares of Pennask Lake Company, Limited stock. However, due to the Depression, there were no new subscribers. In order to keep the Club going, Jim ended up buying another 206 shares, and someone else bought 37 shares.

At the December 31, 1931 annual meeting of Pennask Lake Club stockholders, Jim admitted that he personally was beginning to feel the bite of the depression and appealed to members to buy some of his shares in order to relieve him of the financial burden. He felt that ultimately the Club should be controlled by Canadian citizens. He suggested that the Club buy him out over a period of time. To bring in some money to cut down the Club's operating losses, Jim created a new category of membership, local Associate memberships at $25.00 per year.

The financial situation at the Pennask Lake Club worsened over the course of the depression. Two men came to the rescue, John Milton Hancock and John W. Kieckhefer. Without their support and advice, it is questionable as to whether the Club would have survived. Both men had influential business careers but had time to devote to the Club. Kieckhefer became very active after 1933 and spent a considerable amount of time there. He was said to be Jim's strongest supporter, especially in the area of cost and management control.

After the end of the depression, losses at the Club continued. Few anglers vis-ited the club, and losses mounted. By the end of 1938, only 16 had paid dues. Jim Dole and John Kieckhefer, through a series of advances, loaned the Club nearly $20,000, with $17,000 alone from Jim. Kieckhefer became more involved with the management of the Club, and was optimistic on account of the smaller lakes in the region being fished out. Kieckhefer appealed to Hancock and other members for financial assistance, and was successful in easing the operating strain. However, the Club was not effective in attracting new members. One option was to turn the Pennask Lake Club into a public resort, but the idea was rejected by Jim and others.

Jim then resorted to advertising, a subject he knew all about. Ads were first placed in Time and Field and Stream. These ads did not attract new membership, and the Club continued to financially bleed, even with special donations by members and annual dues. By December 31, 1940, the Club's accumulated deficit totalled $30,500, including advances by Dole and Kieckhefer.

The Club had a few honorary and Associate members, including Norman G. Cull and Earnest H. Adams, Canadians from Vancouver. Of all the 32 Associate memberships granted, 24 were Canadians, which increased to 40 in 1942. These Canadians formed a committee they called a "syndicate" which became very active in the Club's affairs. Cull and E. H. Adams headed the new Canadian Syndicate of Associate members. The Canadian syndicate proposed to inject new capital and acquire control of the Club, assuming they could obtain 75 percent of all the outstanding common stock of The Pennask Lake Company, Limited. The plan would be contingent

Pennask Lake during the good times

on the willingness of both Dole and Kieckhefer to sell their interests to the Canadian syndicate. Together the two owned 70 percent of the outstanding shares. The offer would be made to all the stockholders alike.

The whole idea of the sell-out appealed to Jim because he was concerned that upon his death, the worthless Club shares might present an estate tax problem, plus, his beneficiaries might not be able to convert the unmarketable shares to cash. At the same time, Jim wanted to make sure that his children had privileges to use the Club. Jim had already given his son, James D. Dole, Jr. 15 shares, and he was actively utilizing the Club facilities.

After the lapse of a considerable period of time, it was proposed to stockholders to sell out to the Canadian syndicate for $10 per share, who would also liquidate the debt of the corporation and provide the Club with additional working capital. A condition in the agreement was that the present dues-paying members would have the right to use the Club facilities. The offer was accepted by all parties, and Jim resigned as director of the Club, and received $10 per share for each of the shares that he paid $100 for, plus reimbursement for $9,000 of the loans he and Kieckhefer made to the Club.

The transaction was completed, and the Canadians now controlled the Club with over 80 percent of the outstanding stock. Jim kept 175 shares, and his son, James, Jr. maintained his 15 shares. All the other old-timers were gone. Jim is referred to as the "father of Pennask" at Pennask Lake to this day.

The Club received international attention in the summer of 1959, when Queen Elizabeth II and Prince Philip were taken there for three days. The royal entourage arrived with a staff of twenty-four. While Prince Philip fly fished from shore, the Queen relaxed. On Sunday there was an informal private church service by the Dean of St. Paul's Cathedral, flown in from Kamloops, B.C., which was held in the lodge dining room. On Monday, the Prince and Queen went horseback riding prior to a picnic held on Belle Island.

JIM DOLE'S LEGACY

Jim died in May 1958 after a series of strokes and a heart attack. He is buried in Makawao, on the slopes of Haleakala facing Maui Pineapple company's pineapple fields, at the grave site of Belle's family. Next to Jim is his wife, Belle, who died in November 1972.

Written on Belle's gravestone are the words, "She was Sunshine Joy and Life to All of Us." On Jim's gravestone is inscribed, "He was a Man, Take Him All in All. I Shall Not Look Upon His Like Again."

He is no longer with us, but he left behind a legacy.

He left behind a reputation for honor, integrity and high moral caliber in his business dealings and his life as a whole. What he did for his workers was way ahead of his time.

He left behind the pineapple industry that he had pioneered, and which came to be the second largest industry in the islands, producing in 1930-90 percent of all the canned pineapple produced in the world. The pineapple industry is no longer as important to Hawaii as it was, because other places are canning pineapples successfully and more cheaply, but the cannery he built is one of only two still canning pineapple in Hawaii today. The other one is Maui Pineapple Co., a wholly-owned subsidiary of Maui Land & Pineapple Company, Inc.

He left behind at least two of the companies he had started in California which continue today, James D. Dole Corp. and Chemical Process Company.

He also left behind the Pennask Lake Club, which continues.

He left his name, which had become so identified with quality that is being used more than it ever was when he ran Hapco. Next to "Kraft," "Dole" is the best known brand name today.

His name is now used with products which have nothing to do with pineapples, such as bananas, fresh vegetables, raisins, dates, almonds, pistachios, etc. and with fresh kiwis, lemons and oranges in Japan.

And his name is still associated with pineapples, not only with Dole Hawaii, which packs 225,000 tons, but with Dole Thailand, which packs 200,000 tons of fruit per year and Dole Philippines, which packs 380,000 tons.

Jim's heritage also continues on in his descendants. All his children became respectable members of society. So far they have produced thirteen grandchildren, twenty-one great-grandchildren and one great-great-grandchild. He was good with his grandchildren, who all were very fond of him. It is too bad that he is not still around to be pleased with how well his great-grandchildren have been doing in school and college, and to go to the graduation of the great-grandson who graduated Magna Cum Laude from Harvard, Jim's old alma mater.

When he was getting on in years, Jim liked when he was saying goodbye to someone to say, "Take care of yourself. Good men are scarce. Not many of us left." He was truly a good man and men like him are scarce. He is no longer with us, but his legacy continues on.

Bibliography

Advertiser, The Pacific Commercial, Honolulu, Feb. 9, 1921.

Allen and Chellgard: Honolulu Star-Bulletin, "Lanai Island of Achievement," pp. 4-11, Honolulu, 1926.

Article from unknown Washington, D.C. newspaper, "May Ask the Cabinet Secretary Wilson to Bar Snakes from Hawaii," 1902, found in the personal files of James D. Dole.

Article: "Pineapples," an undated article found in James D. Dole's personal files.

Barnes, K.B. "A Short History of the Pineapple Industry in Hawaii," Hawaiian Pineapple Company, Ltd., 1923.

Beatrice/Hunt-Wesson, various historical information.

Bitting, A.W., M.D. "The Art of Canning; Its History and Development," p. 327–335, The Trade Pressroom, San Francisco, CA, 1937.

Beechert, Edward, Ph.D.: Working in Hawaii – A Labor History, "The Paternalistic Plantation: A New Form of Control," pp. 181-182, and "The Work Force and Welfare Capitalism," p. 243, University of Hawaii Press, 1985.

Bussey Institution: Course Catalog, 1899.

Castle & Cooke, Inc.: Dole-Hawaii Castle & Cooke Foods, A Division of Castle & Cooke, Inc., "Historical Highlights," May 1977.

Castle & Cooke, "Notice of Special Meeting of Shareholders to be held on July 1, 1985, dated June 7, 1988.

Castle & Cooke, 1987 Annual Report to Stockholders.

Castle & Cooke 1988 Proxy Statement.

Castle & Cooke Library: "The Story of Hawaii and Its Builders," pp. 401-404, & 553, 1925; "Men of Hawaii," pp. 33 & 159, 1930; and "Pan Pacific Who's, 1940-41," pp. 178 & 586.

Castle & Cooke Library: Hapco corporate minutes from board of director and stockholder meetings, 1901-1911.

Castle & Cooke Library: Hawaiian Pineapple Company, Ltd., Proxy Statement, Nov. 18, 1903.

Castle & Cooke Library: Managers Report to Stockholders for the period from May 1, 1907 to May 31, 1908.

Castle & Cooke Library: Notes by David W. Eyre, former vice president of public relations of Castle & Cooke

Castle & Cooke Library: Various Castle & Cooke Documents, March 1986.

Castle & Cooke Library: Contract between James D. Dole and Hapco, dated August 30, 1948.

Chapman, Royal N., "Cooperation in the Hawaiian Pineapple Business," p. 6, American Council Institute of Pacific Relations, New York, 1933.

Direct Examination of James D. Dole, In The District Court of the U.S., United States of America (Petitioner) vs. American Can Company and others (Defendants), March 15, 1915.

Dole, Charles F.: The Ethics of Progress, Thomas Y. Crowell & Co., New York, September 1909.

Dole, Charles F.: My Eighty Years, p. 274, E. P. Dutton & Company, New York, 1927.

Dole, Frances D.: "A Plea for Mt. Desert's Forests," Jan.17, 1903, unpublished.

Dole, James D.: Personal Diary: May, 1899 through July 20, 1900, and Sept. 12, 1901.

Dole, James D.: Notes on "Early Interests in Agriculture," undated.

Dole, James D.: "Some Recollections of Twenty-Five Years of the Pineapple Industry," 1926.

Dole, James D.: "Memorandum Regarding Hawaiian Pineapple Company" to the Board of Directors, August 3, 1932.

Dole, James D.: "Impressions of Five Months in Washington," New York Herald-Tribune, April, 1934.

Dole, James D.: "Memo to the Directors of the Hawaiian Pineapple Company, Ltd.," July 20, 1934.

Dole, James D.: "Memorandum Descriptive of Certain Business Activities of Mine Following My Removal from the Position of President and General Manager of the Hawaiian Pineapple Company in 1932, with Particular Reference to My Activities in Connection with Placer Mining Exploration and Developments," 1940.

Dole, James D.: Notes, dated 1931; and March 1, 1955.

Dole, James D.: Notes, dated 1956.

Dole, James D.: "Notes for Autobiography, Chapter II," undated.

Dole, James D.: Notes on "Financing," dated 1931.

Dole, James D.: Notes on "First Visit to Lanai," undated.

Dole, James D.: "History of Hapco," undated.

Dole, James D.: "Notes for Possible Guidance in Framing Up the History of the Hawaiian Pineapple Company, Ltd." undated.

Dole, James D.: Notes on "Starving for Iron," undated.

Dole, James D., Report to Hapco board of directors, Note II, "Some General and Specific Remarks," August 12, 1948.

Dole Packaged Foods, various Documents, including production exhibits.

Dole, W. Herbert: Garden Isle, "How the Doles Came to Hawaii," May 6, 1974.

Encyclopedia Britannica, Volume 17, pp. 184, 840-841; Chicago, 1944.

"Essay by Alta E. Tripp," dated Feb. 24, 1958, unpublished.

"Flight Forms of Dole Flight," dated August 16, 1927.

Forden, Lesley: The Glory Gamblers The Story of the Dole Race, Ch. 2, "Twenty-Five Grand, and Glory," p. 12, Library of Congress, 1986.

Fortune Magazine, "Pineapples in Paradise," pp. 33-35, Nov. 1930.

Hale, Marion Mason: "The Kingdom That Grew Out of A Little Boy's Garden," pp. 6-7, 10, 26-51, Hawaiian Pineapple Company, May 1929.

Hamlet, by William Shakespeare.

Harvard University: 25th. Anniversary Class Report to the Harvard Class of 1899.

Harvard University: Development of Harvard University, 1869-1929, "College Studies."

Harvard University: James D. Dole's Harvard Transcript.

Hawaii Business, "Colin Cameron Takes Over at Maui Pine," pp. 23-28, August 1969.

Hawaii Hochi, "President Dole," August 25, 1926.

Hawaiian Pineapple Company, Ltd.: Advertisements in National Grocers' Trade Magazines, December 1908.

Hawaiian Pineapple Company, Ltd.: Stockholder List, Dec. 4, 1901.

Hawaiian Pineapple Company Ltd.: "By Nature Crowned The King of Fruits," Honolulu, 1927.

Hawaiian Pineapple Company, Ltd.: "What It Means to Grow Big in Twenty-Five Years," Honolulu, 1927.

Hawaiian Pineapple Company, Ltd.: Annual Stockholder reports, 1903-1933.

Hawaiian Pineapple Company, Ltd.: "Statement of Facts Concerning Relationships Between Hawaiian Pineapple Company, Limited and Castle & Cooke, Limited, Part I, Outline History of Hawaiian Pine" pp. 3-28 & Schedule A, Feb. 1, 1943.

Hawaiian Pineapple Packers' Association, "How We Serve Hawaiian Canned Pineapple," Honolulu, 1914.

Hitch, Ph.D., Thomas: The Hawaiian Economy, III. "The Plantation Economy," Pineapple, pp. 241-245, 261-262, and Table I, p. 487a., unpublished manuscript.

Honolulu Advertiser, "Dole in Big Campaign of Advertising," April 13, 1927.

Honolulu Star-Bulletin, "Dole Delivers Cash Prizes to Goebel, Jensen," August 21, 1927.

Honolulu Star-Bulletin, "Place of Dole in the Industry Lauded," 1927.

Honolulu Star-Bulletin, August 17-28, 1928.

Honolulu Star-Bulletin, Jan. 14, 1931.

Horvat, William J.: "Above the Pacific," undocumented article.

Interview of E. W. Jordan by K. B. Barnes of Hapco, in Oct. 1922.

Interview of S. W. Hoyt by Roberts, undated.

Interview of James D. Dole by "Johnny," in 1946.

Interview of Martin Jensen, the only surviving pilot of the Dole Derby, by David Johnson, a former pilot with 3,000 cumulative flight hours, and licenced to fly single engine land planes, in June 1967 (includes parts of undocumented newspaper clippings).

Interview of Inez Gibson by Elizabeth D. Porteus, on March 1, 1982.

Interview of Albert F. Judd, III, by Richard B. Dole, in January 1989.

Interview of Lex Brodie, former Hapco cannery manager, by Richard B. Dole, on January 7, 1989.

Interview of Paul Brewbaker Associate Economist, Bank of Hawaii Economics Dept., by Richard B. Dole, on January 17, 1989.

Interview of Jack Larsen, pineapple industry consultant, by Richard B. Dole, on January 18, 1989.

Interview of Charles H. Dole by Richard B. Dole, on January 30, 1989.

Interview of Deane W. Malott by Richard B. Dole on January 31, 1989

Interview of Elizabeth Dole Porteus by Richard B. Dole, in January 1989.

Interview of James Parker, Director of Agriculture, Dole Foods, by Richard B. Dole, on February 4, 1989.

Interview of Fr. Robert Mackey, by Richard B. Dole, in February 1989.

Interview of Mary Ellen Richardson Nakoa, oldest daughter of Ernest Richardson, a former cowboy at the Koele Ranch, by Richard B. Dole, on February 5, 1989.

Interview of Dwane Black, a former vice president of Castle & Cooke, and current resident of Lanai, by Richard B. Dole, on February 5, 1989.

Interview of Robert L. Hawthorne, vice president and general manager of Dole Packaged Foods Company, Hawaii Division, by Richard B. Dole, on February 13, 1989.

Interview of Edward Beechert, Ph.D., author of **Working in Hawaii – A Labor History,** published in 1985 by University of Hawaii Press, and other books on Hawaii labor history, by Richard B. Dole, on February 14, 1989.

Interview of Nancy Bush, marketing manager, S&W Fine Foods, Inc., by Richard B. Dole, on March 3, 1989.

Interview of Harry Goff by Richard B. Dole, on March 6, 1989.

Interview of Doug Jocelin, Jr., vice president, international, Dole Foods, by Richard B. Dole, on March 6, 1989.

Interview of G. Terry Sharrer, Ph.D., Curator, Division of Agriculture and Natural Resources, National Museum of American History, by Richard B. Dole, on March 9, 1989.

Interview of David Johnson by Richard B. Dole, on March 11, 1989.

Interview of Charles J. Bauman, senior vice president, Dole Food Company, by Richard B. Dole, on March 15, 1989.

Interview of Karen Johnston, public affairs assistant, Beatrice/Hunt/Wesson, by Richard B. Dole, on March 16, 1989.

Interview of Barbara Larsen by Richard B. Dole, on March 16, 1989.

Interview of Joseph Hartley, president of Maui Pineapple Company, on March 21, 1989.

Investment Research Report by **Charles Head & Company,** dated December 1928.

Johnson, David: unpublished manuscript, undated.

Johnson, David: Notes taken from the **San Francisco Examiner,** dated Aug. 19, 1927.

Johnson, David: An unpublished manuscript on the Dole Derby, 1970.

Kula Radio: "Walter Dillingham on Kula Radio," sponsored by W. H.Male, Ltd, Oct. 30, 1949.

Lanai Land and Development Company, "Prospectus," dated December 1896.

Larsen, Barbara: "Memoranda on a Visit to the Dole Farm Home at Wahiawa," June 3, 1958.

Letter to James D. Dole from Mary, dated March 9, 1900.

Letter to James D. Dole from George Dutton, dated Sept. 20, 1900.

Letter to James D. Dole from Fred Mayo, dated Oct. 1900.

Letter to James D. Dole from Page Wheelright, dated Nov. 1900.

Letter to James D. Dole from George Dutton, dated Jan. 1901.

Letter to James D. Dole from Winifred Dole, dated July 1901.

Letter by James D. Dole to Anna Dole, dated July 14, 1901.

Letter to James D. Dole from Winifred Dole, dated August 22, 1901.

Letter to James D. Dole from E. J. Walker, dated October 1, 1901.

Letter from James D. Dole to Anna Dole, dated Feb. 11, 1902.

Letter from James D. Dole to Caroline Dole, dated Oct. 3, 1902.

Letter from James D. Dole to Winifred Dole, dated Dec. 26, 1902.

Letters to James D. Dole from Frances D. Dole, dated Nov. 21, 1902; Nov. 30, 1902; Jan. 9, 1903; and Feb. 13, 1903.

Letter to James D. Dole from George Lurvey, dated Feb. 2, 1903.

Letter to James D. Dole from Charles F. Dole, dated April 30, 1903.

Letters to James D. Dole from Charles F. Dole, dated July 13 & 18, 1903.

Letter from James D. Dole to John Ii Estate, dated Sept. 15, 1903.

Letter to James D. Dole from Phil Tucker, dated Oct. 19, 1903.

Letter to James D. Dole from Phil Tucker, dated Nov. 1, 1903.

Letter to James D. Dole from Charles Bowditch, dated January 12, 1904.

Letter to James D. Dole from Phil Tucker, dated Jan. 31, 1904.

Letters to James D. Dole from Phil Tucker, dated March 4, 1904, March 11, 1904 and July 9, 1904.

Letter to James D. Dole from Edward Brewer, dated July 5, 1904.

Letter to James D. Dole from H. Williams, dated August 10, 1904.

Letter to James D. Dole from George H. Dole, dated July 8, 1905

Letter to James D. Dole from Phil Tucker, dated Oct. 5, 1905.

Letter to James D. Dole from his cousin, Marian Dole Jones, dated August 20, 1906.

Letter from James D. Dole to Belle Dole, dated May 26, 1916.

Letter to the Hapco board of directors by James D. Dole, dated July 20, 1934.

Letter to James D. Dole from Atherton Richards, dated August 31, 1934.

Letter to James D. Dole from Edgar Hagist, dated Sept. 14, 1938.

Letter from James D. Dole to K. B. Barnes, Hapco, dated Jun 13, 1940.

Letter from James D. Dole to the Hapco board of directors, 1948.

Letter from James D. Dole to Kenneth Barnes, Hapco, dated May 3, 1948.

Letter to the Board of Directors of The Schwarz Engineering Company, Inc., "A Tribute to James D. Dole," by Harry Goff, November 16, 1950.

Letter from James D. Dole to C. B. Bayly, dated March 30, 1955.

Letter to Richard B. Dole from Elizabeth Dole Porteus, dated April 10, 1989.

Malott, Deane, vice president, Hapco: "Growth of Pineapple Industry Is Romance of Big Business," **Honolulu Advertiser,** July 2, 1931.

Malott, Deane: Ch. IV, "James D. Dole," Feb. 6, 1988, unpublished.

Maui Land and Pineapple Company, Inc. 1987 SEC Form 10-K; and 1987 Proxy Statement.

Memminger, Charles: **Honolulu Star-Bulletin**, "An Island in Transition," May 3, 1987.

Memo to K. B. Barnes by Abel Rodrigues, July 9, 1948.

Misc. documents from the personal files of James D. Dole.

Murdock, David H., Chairman and Chief Executive Officer Castle & Cooke, Inc., "Castle & Cooke's Global Game Plan," a presentation to the College of Tropical Agriculture and Human Resources University of Hawaii, Convocation Ceremony, on January 8, 1988.

Nedbalek, Lani: **Wahiawa**, "The Pioneers," p.p. 17-24, 27-28, Wonder View Press, 1984.

Nippu Jiji, "Treatment of the Laborers By the Hawaiian Pineapple Company, Ltd.," Dec. 28, 1921.

Noll, Mark A.; Hatch, Nathan O.; Marsden, George M.; Wells, David F.; and Woodbridge, John D. (Editors): **Eerdman's Handbook to Christianity in America**, "Theology and Religious Belief," pp. 228-229, William B. Eerman's Publishing Company, 1983.

Note to James D. Dole from George Dole, dated April 8, 1904.

Notes by S. T. Hoyt, Jan. 15, 1923.

Oehm, Gus. M. : **By Nature Crowned King of Fruits, Pineapple in Hawaii**, pp. 8-17, p. 21, p. 33, pp. 38-95, pp. 121-127, pp. 257-272, pp. 282-293 (Unpublished Manuscript), 1952.

Porteus, Elizabeth D., "The Dole Flight," August 19, 1927, a scrapbook.

Porteus, Elizabeth D.: **Ancestors and Decendents of Wigglesworth Dole From 1639 to 1986**, "The Doles," Part One, Ch. I., pp. 17-20, 27-29 (unpublished manuscript).

Porteus, Elizabeth D.: **Ancestors and Decendents of Wigglesworth Dole From 1639 to 1986**, "The Doles," Part One, Ch. II., pp. 31-32 (unpublished manuscript).

Porteus, Elizabeth D.: **Ancestors and Decendents of Wigglesworth Dole From 1639 to 1986**, "The Doles," Part One, Ch. III., pp. 42-66, 70-71 (unpublished manuscript).

Porteus, Elizabeth D.: **Scrapbook Clipping** (source unknown).

Promissory note from James D. Dole to Charles F. Dole, dated Dec. 26, 1903.

Read, Stanley, E.: "A Place Called Pennask," pp. 1-41, Mitchell Press Limited, Vancouver, Canada, 1977.

Ronch, Ron: **The Honolulu Advertiser**, p. B-2, "Dole Derby," Feb. 2, 1989.

Rossesberry, C. R.: **The Challenging Skies**, "The Doleful Dole Derby," Ch. 10, p. 107, Doubleday & Company, New York, 1966.

S & W Product Information brochure, undated; Various historical data provided by S & W.

Simmonds, N. W., Editor: **Evolution of Crop Plants**, "Pineapple," Barbara Pickersgill, University of Reading, Reading, England, pp. 14-17, 1976 by Longman, London and New York.

Tape by Barbara Dole, dated 1973.

Taylor, Frank: **The Reader's Digest**, "Billion-Dollar Rainbow," December 1954.

Taylor, Frank; Welty, Earl M.; and Eyre, David W.: **From Land and Sea, The Story of Castle & Cooke of Hawaii**, "Incorporation," pp. 164-165, and p. 280, Chronicle Publishing Company, 1976.

Wahiawa Pineapple Co., Ltd.: "Prospectus," dated June 30, 1904.

The Water Tower, "Elevated Tank Advertises Hawaiian Pineapple," January 1929.

Western Canner, "Pineapple," June 1934.

Western Investor, "Hawaiian Securities Digest," Summer 1985 & Summer 1987.

White, Henry A.: "James D. Dole, Industrial Pioneer of the Pacific," p. 9 & pp. 21-27, New York: Newcomen Society in North America, June 1957.